Robotic Process Automation with Blue Prism Quick Start Guide

Create software robots and automate bus. ss processes

Lim Mei Ying

BIRMINGHAM - MUMBAI

Robotic Process Automation with Blue Prism Quick Start Guide

Copyright © 2018 Packt Publishing

Commissioning Editor: Douglas Paterson
Acquisition Editor: Siddharth Mandal
Content Development Editor: Smit Carvalho
Technical Editor: Sushmeeta Jena
Copy Editor: Safis Editing
Project Coordinator: Hardik Bhinde
Proofreader: Safis Editing
Indexer: Rekha Nair
Graphics: Alishon Mendonsa
Production Coordinator: Priyanka Dhadke

First published: November 2018

Production reference: 1301118

Published by Packt Publishing Ltd.
Livery Place
35 Livery Street
Birmingham
B3 2PB, UK.

ISBN 978-1-78961-044-4

www.packtpub.com

`mapt.io`

Mapt is an online digital library that gives you full access to over 5,000 books and videos, as well as industry leading tools to help you plan your personal development and advance your career. For more information, please visit our website.

Why subscribe?

- Spend less time learning and more time coding with practical eBooks and Videos from over 4,000 industry professionals

- Improve your learning with Skill Plans built especially for you

- Get a free eBook or video every month

- Mapt is fully searchable

- Copy and paste, print, and bookmark content

Packt.com

Did you know that Packt offers eBook versions of every book published, with PDF and ePub files available? You can upgrade to the eBook version at `www.packt.com` and as a print book customer, you are entitled to a discount on the eBook copy. Get in touch with us at `customercare@packtpub.com` for more details.

At `www.packt.com`, you can also read a collection of free technical articles, sign up for a range of free newsletters, and receive exclusive discounts and offers on Packt books and eBooks.

Contributors

About the author

Lim Mei Ying has extensive experience in designing, implementing and supporting Blue Prism processes as well as setting up a Robotic Operating Model for the enterprise. She has spent many hours figuring out the dos and don'ts of Blue Prism technologies and thrives on the challenge of finding new ways to solve automation problems. Mei Ying lives on the sunny island of Singapore.

About the reviewer

Saibal Goswami has a career spanning more than 12 years, during which time he has developed a strong competency in partnership management, client relationships, project management, business analysis, and operations management. He cultivated these competencies through an efficient process-feasibility study, cost/benefit analyses, resource planning, and leading and mentoring cross-functional teams in order to maximize productivity. Saibal has been associated with RPA from the very beginning. He has mastered various technical skills, including RPA process assessment and RPA CoE.

Packt is searching for authors like you

If you're interested in becoming an author for Packt, please visit authors.packtpub.com and apply today. We have worked with thousands of developers and tech professionals, just like you, to help them share their insight with the global tech community. You can make a general application, apply for a specific hot topic that we are recruiting an author for, or submit your own idea.

Table of Contents

Preface

Recently robotics process automation has been growing increasingly popular. The arrival of robotic process tools, such as Blue Prism, has opened up a world of opportunities. Processes that could not be automated previously may now be automated. These may include processes that involve legacy applications that no one dares to upgrade for fear that something may break. Or perhaps the application came from a shrink-wrapped box and it does not provide any means for developers to extend and integrate.

In the past, the only way to get the job done was for a human to perform mundane data entry, point-and-click operations. Now platforms like Blue Prism are able to simulate exactly what humans do without the need for costly system enhancements and change requests. You just need to train the robot to mimic what the human does and the process gets automated!

The best part is, you don't have to be overly technical to build a process from the ground up. The book was written to build a single process up from scratch. While building the process, the reader is taken step by step through all the basic functions of Blue Prism, from creating a process, to building up an object and using frequently used applications such as Excel and Outlook.

Who this book is for

The idea behind this book was to help out people who may not be very technical to build their own processes. At my previous place of work, we worked extensively with end users to help automate their processes. Because the direction at that time was for end users to be the developers, we witnessed many people struggling to get the basics right. They were not trained in computer science 101, they had no concept of what a loop or collection is, and so on. And there they were, sitting in the room with us, trying to get their processes to work. They had been through the in-house foundation training but, for some reason, some of the concepts didn't stick. They really needed help to meet their deadlines.

Think of this book as that special coach sitting next to you as you build your process to help you get past the tricky bits. In this book, we have collected the experience from all these consultation sessions, collecting all the frequently asked questions to help you navigate the pitfalls of process building.

What this book covers

Chapter 1, *The Case for Robotic Process Automation*, gives some background on what robotic process automation is, and what processes are best suited for automation, as well as a brief overview of the robotic process operation model.

Chapter 2, *Building the First Blue Prism Process*, takes the reader through the creation of a simple process.

Chapter 3, *Pages, Data Items, Blocks, Collections, and Loops*, continues to build on the process by adding pages, data items, blocks, collections, and loops.

Chapter 4, *Actions, Decisions, Choices, and Calculations*, explores the use of actions, decisions, choices, and calculations in building the process.

Chapter 5, *Implementing Business Objects*, shows how to teach the robot to interact with applications such as Internet Explorer.

Chapter 6, *Spying Elements*, looks at spying elements, which are used to identify what the robot needs to interact with on the screen.

Chapter 7, *Write, Wait, and Read*, builds the logic behind the business object by using read, write, and wait stages.

Chapter 8, *Working with Excel*, covers reading and writing to Excel and CSV files.

Chapter 9, *Sending and Receiving Emails*, explains how to read and send emails using Outlook.

Chapter 10, *Control Room and Work Queues*, introduces the control room, adding items to a queue, processing the items, and updating the work status.

Chapter 11, *Exception Handling*, demonstrates how to handle errors that are both expected and unexpected in a graceful manner.

To get the most out of this book

We don't assume that you have any programming experience. All you need is the willingness to learn and a process to automate.

Download the example code files

You can download the example code files for this book from your account at
`www.packt.com`. If you purchased this book elsewhere, you can visit
`www.packt.com/support` and register to have the files emailed directly to you.

You can download the code files by following these steps:

1. Log in or register at `www.packt.com`.
2. Select the **SUPPORT** tab.
3. Click on **Code Downloads & Errata**.
4. Enter the name of the book in the **Search** box and follow the onscreen instructions.

Once the file is downloaded, please make sure that you unzip or extract the folder using the latest version of:

- WinRAR/7-Zip for Windows
- Zipeg/iZip/UnRarX for Mac
- 7-Zip/PeaZip for Linux

The code bundle for the book is also hosted on GitHub at `https://github.com/PacktPublishing/Robotic-Process-Automation-with-Blue-Prism-Quick-Start-Guide`. In case there's an update to the code, it will be updated on the existing GitHub repository.

We also have other code bundles from our rich catalog of books and videos available at `https://github.com/PacktPublishing/`. Check them out!

Download the color images

We also provide a PDF file that has color images of the screenshots/diagrams used in this book. You can download it here: `https://www.packtpub.com/sites/default/files/downloads/9781789610444_ColorImages.pdf`.

Get in touch

Feedback from our readers is always welcome.

General feedback: If you have questions about any aspect of this book, mention the book title in the subject of your message and email us at `customercare@packtpub.com`.

Errata: Although we have taken every care to ensure the accuracy of our content, mistakes do happen. If you have found a mistake in this book, we would be grateful if you would report this to us. Please visit www.packt.com/submit-errata, selecting your book, clicking on the Errata Submission Form link, and entering the details.

Piracy: If you come across any illegal copies of our works in any form on the internet, we would be grateful if you would provide us with the location address or website name. Please contact us at copyright@packt.com with a link to the material.

If you are interested in becoming an author: If there is a topic that you have expertise in, and you are interested in either writing or contributing to a book, please visit authors.packtpub.com.

Reviews

Please leave a review. Once you have read and used this book, why not leave a review on the site that you purchased it from? Potential readers can then see and use your unbiased opinion to make purchase decisions, we at Packt can understand what you think about our products, and our authors can see your feedback on their book. Thank you!

For more information about Packt, please visit packt.com.

1
The Case for Robotic Process Automation

Have you ever wondered what it would be like to have a clone? Someone to sit at your desk in the office to do all the tedious, mundane, and monotonous work? The reality of getting a robot to do tasks that were previously done by humans is now made possible by robotic process automation.

Robotic process automation is not a new concept. For years, people have been programming scripts to download data from websites, macros to automate spreadsheets, and recorders to record mouse-clicks. Whatever could be done by a computer could be fulfilled somehow or other in the hands of a highly skilled programmer. However, it is only recently where all these capabilities have been built into a product. And to top it off, the tools enable citizen developers to build their own processes without the technical complexity of writing oodles of code lines.

In this chapter, we will start at square one. We will take a look at what robotic process automation is all about and we will perform a quick study to pick out a process suited for RPA. The topics covered in this chapter are the following:

- What is robotic process automation?
- Finding a process suitable for automation
- The process definition document

What is robotic process automation?

In recent times, RPA's popularity has been on the rise. The main selling point for the adoption of a robotic workforce is the reduction in cost. Given the right processes, a trained robot can mimic the same function as its human counterpart. It does not sleep, go on vacations, or take sick leave. It does not complain about overtime or require a heart-to-heart chat over performance evaluations. The cost of maintaining a robot is generally cheaper than hiring a human employee. In addition, the robot can perform repetitive tasks, freeing up the human to take on more value-added work.

Robotic process automation is a software robot. You won't actually see a physical machine with arms, legs, and wheels tapping away on a keyboard. With the help of a software program, a robot trainer records keystrokes and mouse clicks. These actions are replayed by a computer (the robot) to mimic the actions of a human.

For example, perhaps the trainer would like the robot to scan a shopping site to purchase weekly groceries.

As a human, these are the steps that he would take to purchase a box of cereal:

1. Visit his favorite shopping site: `http://www.amazon.com`
2. Enter the name of the cereal into the search box and click the **Search** button
3. Pick out the box of cereal that he wants to buy

The robot would perform the same task in the following way:

1. Open the browser with the start address of `http://www.amazon.com`.
2. Identify the location of the **Search** box. Send keystrokes to key in the name of the cereal.
3. Identify the location of the **Search** button. Press the button.
4. Identify the location of the search results.
5. Based on a pre-determined algorithm, click on the desired item in the list, for example, it could simply be the first search result on the list.

The robot will store all these instructions within the software program. When requested, it will repeat what it was told to key in and enter step-by-step. It is for this reason that processes selected for robotic automation have to be repeatable.

There is no inherent intelligence. It will do exactly what the trainer tells it to do. The robot will not be able to *see* that there is an ongoing promotion from Shop B where they sell two boxes for the price of three. It will always pick the first item in the search results. Similarly, if the cereal has been discontinued by the manufacturer, the robot will faithfully try to search for it and purchase it. It won't automatically switch to an alternative flavor or brand. There are advances in the industry to add cognitive intelligence to RPA robots. Algorithms such as natural language processing, text analytics, and data mining are used together with RPA to produce robots that are able to respond to situations intelligently and not just based on what it has been told to do by the trainer. However, these are still emerging technologies. The kind of automation that robots do in RPA are usually the repeatable type that has predictable inputs and outputs.

Finding a process suitable for automation

There are many jobs that we do on a day-to-day basis that are repetitive. We may not realize it, but many knowledge workers today are performing tasks that are tedious, routine, and monotonous. Perhaps some of the following tasks may sound familiar to you:

- Visiting a variety of websites to download reports. Followed by extracting information from each report and compiling the data into a spreadsheet for further analysis, reporting, and then emailing the consolidated report to your manager.
- Checking your email for alerts and notifications. Reading the email and if it says *act on this*, you go to another system to key in an order or perform a transaction. Rinse and repeat for the remaining 100 emails in the inbox.
- Downloading a report from a central dashboard and comparing the thousands of rows in the Excel with that of a master copy for discrepancies.
- Basic data entry—entering rows and rows of data into a system.

The good news is, most of these tasks can be done reliably and repeatably by a software robot.

Identifying a process that is suitable for automation may turn out to be more of an art than science. While robots can be trained to perform just about any software-related job, not everything is suited for RPA.

The ideal process for RPA is one that has the following characteristics:

- **No abstract decision making**: The robot is going to do exactly what you tell it to do. Therefore, whatever process that you decide to automate, it's got to work the same way over and over again. If you program it to purchase a chocolate cake with cherries on the top, it's going to do that each time it runs. It's not going to suddenly decide that the weather has been hot lately and that the client may want a chocolate sundae instead (unless you tell it to).

- **Requires no human intervention**: The moment that you need a human to perform steps within the process, chances are, you won't be able to automate it fully. Some examples of this include steps that require a wet-ink signature or read off a physical token. You still can automate processes that have human elements in them, just not completely (also known as **assisted automation**).

- **Repeatable**: The robot is going to take the same series of steps each time it runs. Given the same inputs, the process will deliver the same outputs. While you can put a certain amount of rules into the flow, the results have to be predictable and repeatable for the robot to function correctly.

- **Takes up a considerable amount of time to run manually**: Getting the robot to run a process that takes five minutes to complete daily equates to more time savings than that of a process that takes five minutes to run annually. Go for the processes that yield higher time savings.

- **Interacts with systems that do not get updated unexpectedly**: One of the greatest strengths of robots is their ability to work with most applications, even legacy types. They can read screens, write to text boxes, and click most types of buttons. However, the training the robot receives to perform these actions is only good if the screen that it was trained to understand does not change. Should, for example, the application owner decide to introduce a new mandatory field to the form, the robot will have to be re-trained to understand the new field. Therefore, choose processes that work with applications that are not prone to changes. Ideally, one that you can anticipate the changes when it gets updated (which is easy to do if you or your organization is the owner) so that you have ample time to re-train the robot. Applications that are owned by others, like those on the internet, may change at will, and cause your process to go awry unexpectedly.

- **Requires accuracy, especially when performing data-entry**: Humans tend to make typos when keying data. If you have worked with any forms that deal with money, you would know that simply moving a decimal place in a number can be fatal. Even misspelling an address or postal code can result in a missing shipment and a bad customer experience. Robots will not make these types of mistakes, and therefore can be trusted with processes that require a high level of accuracy in data-entry.

- **Timeliness is important**: Robots can be tasked to look for emails or read a database 24x7. That means the moment an order comes in, even in the wee hours of the night, the robot can process it rather than waiting for a human to report to work the next day to do the job.

As with any project, employing a robot to take over a human process has various other soft points to consider, in addition to the ones above. For example, the willingness of the process owner to embrace change, budget and funding, whether or not the bosses are all aligned with the vision, and so on. Or you might just dive into automating the simplest process first, even if at first it doesn't give the biggest savings. At the end of the day, robots will keep the savings going and going. As long as the process is relevant, and the robot is working, the numbers will keep adding up. The work and value that the robot gives back to the organization will grow cumulatively.

Calculating time savings

If you are looking for that perfect process to automate, you would typically start with a chat with the business users to take an inventory of all the processes that they currently own. List them in a spreadsheet, and put down all the key considerations in a weighted list. There will probably be a shortlist of potentials, and there will likely be several discussions with the user on which process provides the greatest automation value.

To help, you might have a spreadsheet that records the steps in each manual process, and the time taken to execute each step as shown in the following diagram. If we add the estimated time to complete the task of searching the item, purchasing the item, tracking the package, and receiving it—the weekly purchase of groceries takes around 2709 minutes per year of our time:

Process Name: Weekly purchase of groceries					
No.	Step	Frequency	Type of task	Average Handling time	Total Time Savings/year
1	Search for the item.	Weekly	Repetitive	10 minutes	520 minutes
2	Purchase the item	Weekly	Repetitive	5 minutes	260 minutes
3	Track the package	Daily	Repetitive	5 minutes	1825 minutes
4	Receive the package	Weekly	Manual	2 minutes	104 minutes
				Total time saved/year	2709 minutes

The total amount of timed saved per year for each process is then collated into a master spreadsheet as shown in the following screenshot. We've added a few more fictitious processes into the list just to give you an idea of what the list may look like:

Process Name	Total Savings/year (minutes)
Weekly purchase of groceries	2709
Paying electrical bills	421
Checking credit card statements against scanned receipts	1205
Entering name cards into Outlook contacts list	289

From the consolidated list, you will get a better idea of which processes to shortlist as candidates that will deliver the biggest time savings when automated. In this little demonstration, it appears that the weekly purchase of groceries would be an ideal candidate for automation.

The process definition document

Once you have decided which process to automate, we will create a **process definition document (PDD)**. Don't be daunted by the thought of doing documentation. The PDD is simply a place to write down exactly what the robot should be doing, step-by-step. Think of the robot as a new trainee and you will need to pass it the manual on how to perform this task. If you already have a manual, you can re-use it. Otherwise, even doing a simple one at this point will help organize your thought processes later when you build the process.

The PDD typically contains the following sections:

- Manual process description and target systems
- Process diagram
- Process details
- Exceptions

Let's walk through each section in detail for the weekly purchase of groceries process that we will be building.

Manual process description and target systems

To start off, we will capture the high level description of the process. In our example, we could write the following:

- A shopping list is drawn up based on what we need for the upcoming week
- We log on to the shopping site, `http://www.amazon.com`, every Monday at 10:00 am in the morning
- One-by-one, we work through the shopping list and search for the items to purchase
- The item is added to the shopping cart
- An email alert is sent to me for verification and to check out the item

Here, we will also note the systems that we are going to work with. In this case, that will be the shopping site, `http://www.amazon.com` as well as Excel, for storing the shopping list, and Outlook for sending out emails.

Process diagram

Next, we will draw out the process diagram, which is really a pictorial way to show what the process does in the form of a flow chart.

The flow chart always has a start and end point that is typically depicted by two ovals. In between, add the steps of the process inside rectangles. You do not have to put in the details of each step; that will be done in the next section.

The process starts by getting the list of items to purchase. We then work through the list one-by-one by launching the shopping website, search for the item and add it to the cart. After the operation is done, we close the website.

We also have a decision diamond to decide whether or not there are more items to purchase. If there are, we loop back to get the next item to purchase. Once everything has been added to the cart, we send an email notification to inform someone to check out the items and complete the purchase.

The following diagram shows what the flow chart looks like:

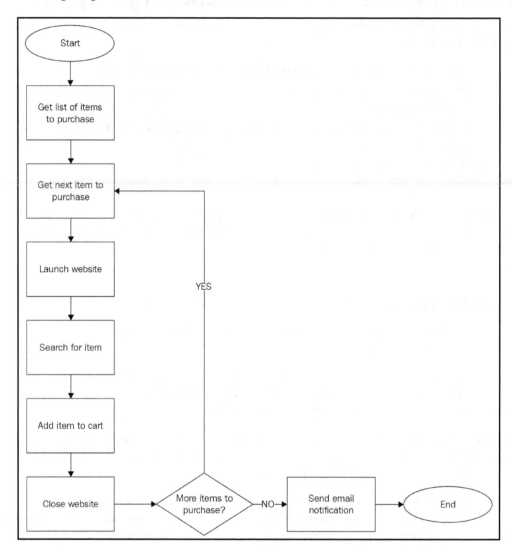

Process details

There are several ways of recording the process details. This is the section that often goes out of date very quickly and is also the most difficult to capture correctly. One way is to take a screenshot of each step in the process and write down which buttons to click, what to enter in each text box, etc. Please see the following example:

- **Get list of items to purchase**: Before starting the purchase, look up the list written in the Excel spreadsheet titled `Shopping List`.
- **Searching for item to purchase**: Search for the item by following the steps shown here:

  - Open **Internet Explorer**. Navigate to `http://www.amazon.com`.
  - Go to the search box at the top of the page. Enter the keywords that match the item to purchase.
  - Click the **Search** button:

- **Choose the item to purchase**: When the search results appear, we pick the one we want to purchase:

  - Scan through the search results.
  - Click on the first item on the list that matches the description that is not a sponsored product:

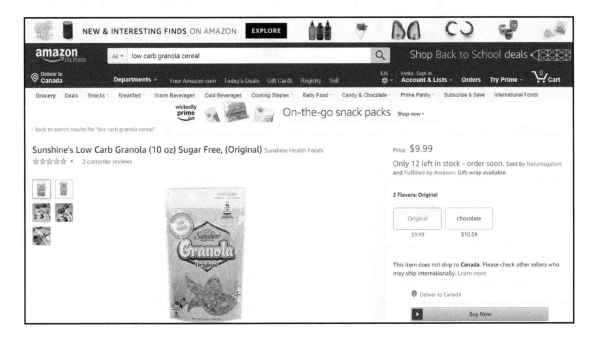

As you can imagine, this is a very detailed way of documenting the entire process. Every mouse-click, keyboard entry, dialog, and pop-up are meticulously recorded here. The more details that you provide in this section, the better. It's just like a movie script that tells you exactly what to do each step of the way. Ideally, you can pass this set of instructions to anyone and they will be able to perform the task for you as if you were doing it yourself.

Sometimes, it gets too tedious to write everything down. Alternatively, consider capturing the details by recording it into a movie. Have the subject matter expert execute the task, and do a live recording with a screen movie capture tool. A voice commentary while he/she clicks through the screens will serve as a form of documentation for the thought processes behind each click.

Exceptions

We'd like to think that the robot will always get it right the first time. However, remember that the robot will only do what you tell it to do. If it meets an unknown situation, like if the item is out of stock, it will not know how to respond and will terminate the process.

It's not too early to think of all the what-ifs that could happen when executing the process. Writing it down in this section will help us to plan out the design of the process better and train the robot to gracefully deal with as many unknowns as you can think of at this point.

For example, exceptions that could possibly happen in our little grocery purchasing process could include the following:

- The item that we are looking for cannot be found
- The item that we are looking for is out-of-stock

In this case, we would probably get the robot to note down which items it is not able to add to the basket and mail us a list at the end of the process.

Summary

In this chapter we learnt what robotic process automation is and how it can be applied to automate the tedious and repeatable work we do in our jobs every day.

We did a simple (albeit fictional) discovery exercise on how to identify processes suitable for automation. Once we selected the process to automate, we learnt to write a process design document to help shape our thoughts before we start coding it.

Now that we have the process design document done, we are ready to take a look at Blue Prism, the tool that we will be using in this book.

Building the First Blue Prism Process

2

With the increased popularity of RPA comes a multitude of products that offer robotic process automation solutions. The tool used in this book is Blue Prism. Blue Prism was founded on July 16, 2001 by a group of process automation experts, and has its headquarters in the United Kingdom. It has been well received, with hundreds of companies (a number that is growing rapidly) around the world adopting Blue Prism as their robotic software of choice.

In this chapter, we will take a look at Blue Prism and use it to build our very first process. Here's what we will be doing:

- Learning how to launch the Blue Prism interactive client
- Using Studio to create our very first process
- Editing the process by giving the robot instructions to follow
- Renaming and saving the process
- And finally, running the process for the first time

Inside a Blue Prism system

In its simplest form, the Blue Prism software is made up of three components:

- The **Application Server** that runs the Blue Prism services. It serves as the *brain* of the entire setup, performing functions such as connecting to the backend databases, scheduling, and storing logs.

- The **Runtime Resource**, which are more commonly known as the robots. They can be either physical or virtual computers.
- The **Interactive Client** installed on your desktop that allows humans to interact with the robots by developing processes, scheduling tasks, or monitoring the robot logs.

The three components pass information to each other on a constant basis in order to make the entire system work as shown in following diagram:

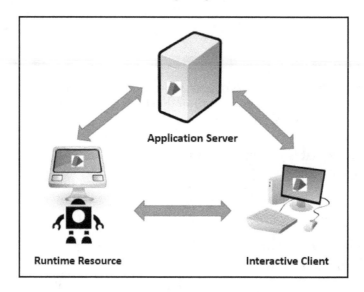

In this book, we will assume that the application server, runtime resources, and the interactive clients have been configured correctly by a system administrator. If you need to perform the installation of the software yourself, do refer to the Blue Prism user guide—Installing v6.0 for local training guide on the Blue Prism portal (`https://portal.blueprism.com/user/login?destination=/documents/blue-prism-user-guide-installing-v60-local-training`).

As a robot trainer/developer, you probably won't see much of the application server or the runtime resource. The tool that you will work with almost exclusively is the **Interactive Client**. The Blue Prism interactive client is the main software that will be used in the development of robotic processes.

This book uses Blue Prism version 6.3. If you are using other versions of the product, the screen grabs may differ somewhat.

Launching the Blue Prism interactive client

Once you have successfully installed the Blue Prism interactive client, you can launch it in any of the following ways:

- From the **Start Menu,** click **Start** | **Blue Prism**.
- Alternatively, you may choose **Run** | **Blue Prism**

The Blue Prism application is represented by a blue triangle. Double-click on the icon to open it.

A sign-in screen appears. Follow these steps to sign in:

1. Choose the connection that your Blue Prism administrator has configured for you.
2. If you see a **User Name** and **Password** field, enter your Blue Prism credentials. This is an account that has been issued to you by your Blue Prism administrator. It is not your Windows username and password.
3. When done, click the **Sign In** button.

 You won't always see the **User Name** and **Password** fields. These only appear if single sign-on has not been turned on in your environment. If your Blue Prism administrator intends for you to use the same credentials as those you use to log onto Windows, only the **Connection** field will be visible.

The five tabs at the top menu bring you each of the modules available in Blue Prism. These five menu items are also available as buttons on the left navigation bar, as shown on the following screen. Click on each of them to see what shows up:

- **Studio**: This button provides a directory listing of all the processes and objects available in Blue Prism.
- **Control**: This is the place to schedule processes or run them on demand.
- **Dashboard**: The information shown here is the same as that of the home page. You can also create additional dashboards and view them from here.
- **Releases**: This is where you would go to create deployment packages or to import a package created in another environment.
- **System**: Contains all the configurable settings that you can set. As a developer, you would use this frequently to set environment variables, as demonstrated in the following screenshot:

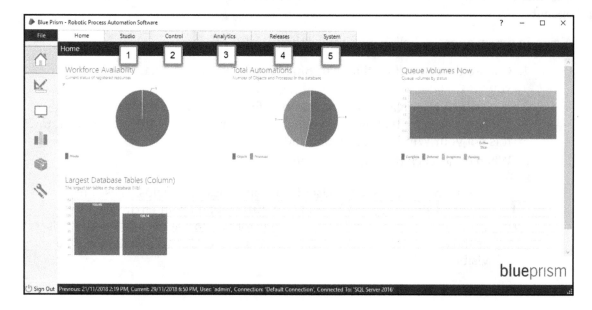

The footer at the bottom of the page contains the following bits of information, as shown in the following list of bullet points. The name of the connection becomes particularly important when you work with multiple Blue Prism environments. A typical scenario is to have an environment for development, another for quality testing, and a third for production. You would not want to unwittingly make changes to production that were meant for development, so it's always a good idea to check these values before making any changes:

- Previous logged-on time
- Current logged-on time
- Account that was used to log in
- The name of the connection
- The name of the database to which you are connected:

Creating the first process

As developers, we will be spending most of our time with Studio. This is the place where we work with processes/objects.

Let's dive right in and create our first process:

1. Click on the **Studio** button. The screen shows a tree on the left-hand side. The tree contains two leaf nodes at the top: **Processes** and **Objects**.
2. Right-click on **Processes** and choose **Create Process**.
3. The **New Process** dialog appears. Give the new process a name. Call it **My First Process**. Click **Next.**

4. Enter an optional description for the process. It's always a good idea to write a bit about what we are going to build so that others will know what the process is doing. For now, just provide a token description, for example: **This is my first Blue Prism process**. When you are ready, click **Finish**.

5. The process shows up in the tree on the left, inside a folder named **Default**.

Look at the panel on the right (refer to the following screenshot). It shows the date and time the process was created and who created it. Later on, as you edit the process, the list will grow to become an audit trail of who has edited the process and when:

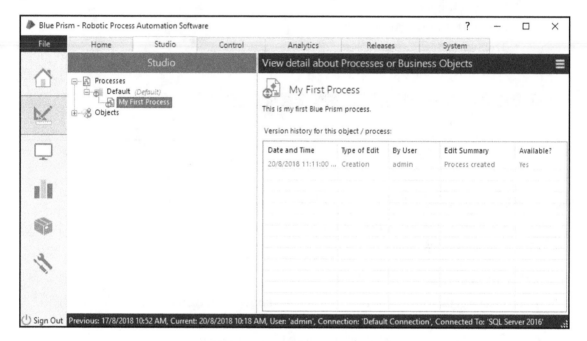

6. From the tree, double-click on the newly created process. The process opens for editing in a canvas in Process Studio.

Getting to know the Blue Prism Process Studio

Most RPA programs today are code-free (or at least low code), and Blue Prism is no different. It provides a Visio-like canvas to sequence each step in the process. You design a flowchart that contains a sequence of steps. You can choose from a suite of ready-made actions what each step is supposed to do (for example, click a link or press a button). Finally, the steps are linked together with a definite start and endpoint.

Let's take a quick tour of what it's comprised of:

- **Top menu** has all the commands and tasks that we will need to create our processes.
- **Toolbar** gives us quick access to commonly used commands and tasks.
- **Toolbox** contains the ready-to-use actions that you can drag and drop onto the canvas.
- **Canvas** is where we will draw the process flow diagram. Also notice that the first and only page that we have opened is called **Main Page**. This is the starting point for all processes. In the canvas as shown in the following screenshot, we see three things:
    - A **Start** oval represents the starting point of the process
    - An **End** oval represents the endpoint of the process

- A **Page Information** block provides a name and description of the process, as well as the preconditions and post conditions. This information is used solely for documentation purposes. It will be available in the auto-generated help file when someone looks up your process in Blue Prism Studio, as demonstrated in the following screenshot:

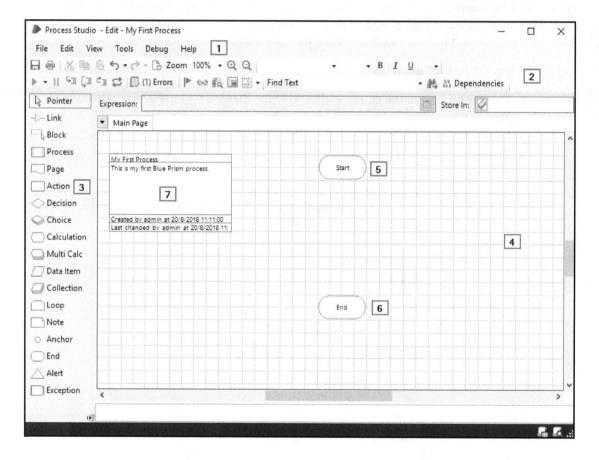

Adding pages

Now, let's do a simple exercise and start to shape out our little purchasing process by adding more pages to it:

1. From the toolbox, click on ⬜Page . Drag and drop the page stage to the canvas.
2. In the dialog that appears, choose **Add a new page and create a reference to it**. Click **Next**.
3. Give a name to the page. Let's call it **Get List of items to purchase**. Click **Finish**.
4. The page object is added to the canvas as shown in the following screenshot. In addition, a new page is added to the process. It shows up just above the canvas as an additional tab:

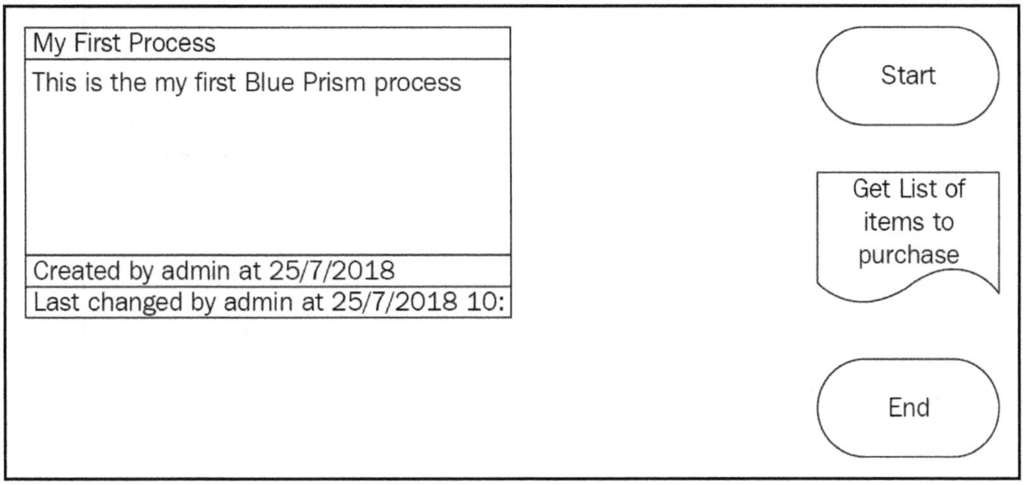

My First Process
This is the my first Blue Prism process
Created by admin at 25/7/2018
Last changed by admin at 25/7/2018 10:

Start

Get List of items to purchase

End

5. Let's add a couple more pages to the process. Drag two more page stages to the canvas. Give them the following titles:
   - **Search and Add Item to Cart**
   - **Send Email Notification**

The screenshot should now look as follows:

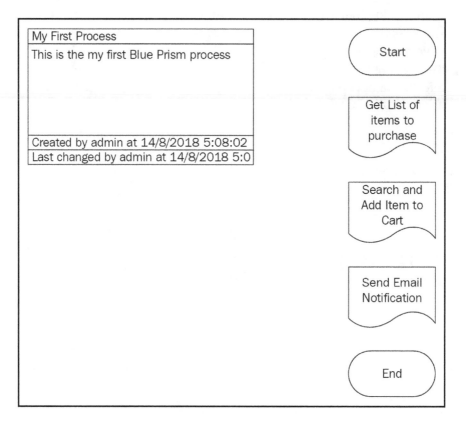

6. From the toolbox, click ⊢Link . Notice that the pointer changes to that of an arrow with a link ↘⊹ . Use it to link up all the stages together from **Start** to **End**. The completed diagram is as follows:

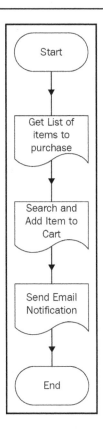

Editing pages

We added three pages to the process. However, they are all blank since we have not coded anything in them. Let's add stubs to each page so that the process is complete. As we work through the book, we will fill up each page with the actual task that they are supposed to carry out:

1. Click on the **Get List of Items to Purchase** tab. The page was automatically created when we added the page block to the main page. At this point, it is completely empty, except for a **Start** and **End** block.

2. From the toolbox, drag and drop a block between the **Start** and **End** blocks. Double-click on the newly added block and write something in the **Node Text** section, for example, **TODO: Add the logic on how to get the list of items to purchase**. Click **OK** when done to close the dialog.

3. Use the **Link** tool from the toolbox to link up all the stages. The completed page should appear as follows:

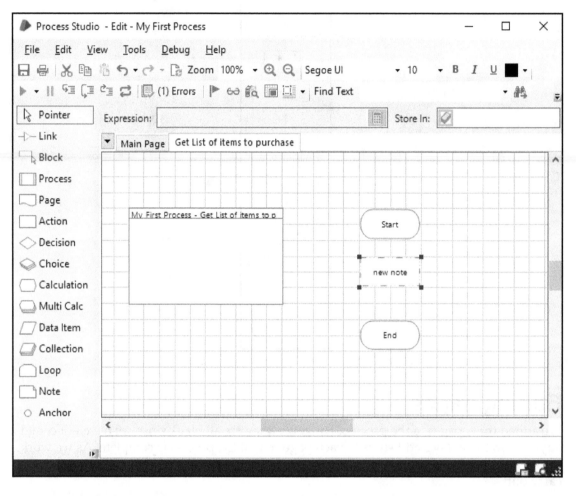

4. Repeat the preceding steps for the remaining two pages that we created earlier.

And we are done! We may not have added much logic to the process yet. We will do so in the coming chapters. As of now, our little process has just the skeletal parts linked up together.

Renaming a process

We started off by naming the process **My First Process**. It is time to give it a name to better reflect what it is doing. Here's how you can go about renaming the process:

1. Go back to the main page.
2. Double-click the page information box.
3. Give the process a new name and description. We are naming the process **Weekly purchase of groceries**, as shown in the following dialog:

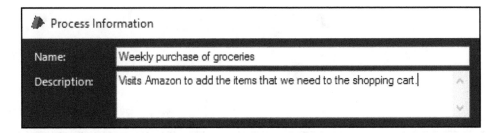

4. Click **OK** to close the dialog. Save the process for the changes to take effect.

Saving a process

It's always a good idea to save your work from time to time. Besides, Blue Prism requires you to save a process before you can run it for the first time. To save the process, click on the **Save** button from the toolbar.

You may, or may not, get the following prompt that requests a number of notes before you can save. If you do, simply add some descriptive text to explain what changes have been made to the process. What you enter here appears in the version history of the process. Click **Save Changes** when done:

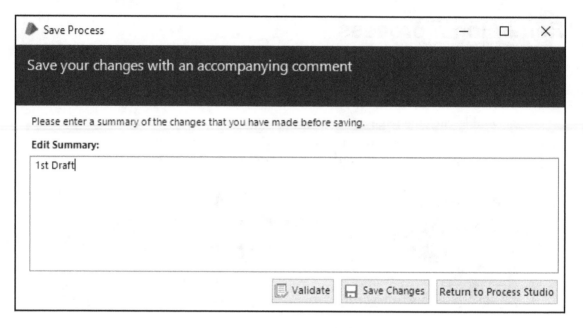

Running the process for the first time

Now, let's give our little process a run. To run it, click the **Go** button from the toolbar. Look for the button with the green triangle and click on it.

The Blue Prism Studio steps through each action block one by one. The action that it is currently executing is highlighted in orange.

If all goes well, you should see the process move from **Start** to the page blocks, and then all the way to the end, with the final stage highlighted as shown in the following screenshot:

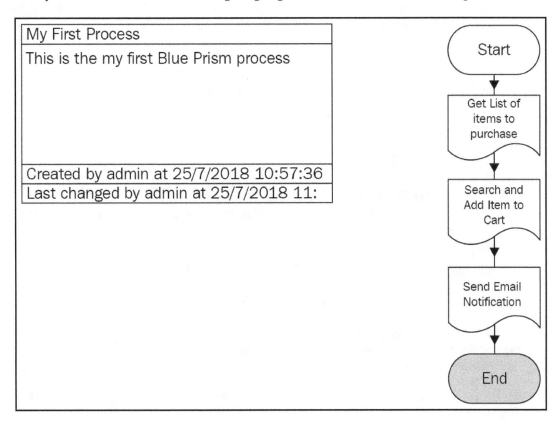

You can re-run the process any time. Simply press the reset button ⮂ from the toolbar and press the **Go** button again.

The robot steps through each stage at a comfortable pace. You can make it go faster or slower by adjusting the speed. Take a look at the **Play** button. Do you notice that it has a

little down arrow next to it, ▶ ▾ ? Click on the arrow and a speed bar appears. Adjust the speed to be faster or slower by dragging the meter up or down. Try dragging the meter all the way to the top so that the speed is at its fastest. Run the process again and watch the robot move at the fastest speed.

Stepping through the process

Clicking **Go** gets the robot to run through the entire process without any planned stops. To execute the process in a more controlled manner, you can use the following buttons on the toolbar:

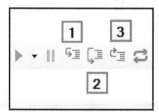

- **Step** (*F11*) **(1)**: Walks through each stage of the process individually and pauses at each stage. When it lands on a sub-page, it will step through the stages of the sub-page.
- **Step Over** (*Shift + F11*) **(2)**: Behaves the same as **Step**. However, when it lands on a page, it will not open up the page, but execute it as a single unit.
- **Step Out** (*F10*) **(2)**: While stepping through a sub-page, use **Step Out** to complete the execution of the sub-page in order to return to the calling page.

You could also run to a specific stage by right-clicking on the stage and choosing the **Run to this Stage** option from the context menu. There is also an option to start from a specific stage in the process by selecting **Set Next Stage**.

Let's run the process again. This time, we will control the robot by stepping through the following stages:

1. From the toolbar, press **Reset** ⮂ .

2. Press **Step** ⤵ . Notice that the robot begins from the first stage directly after **Start**. In our case, that is **Get List of items to purchase**.

3. Remember that when **Step** lands on a sub-page, it will open it up and walk through it. Press **Step** again. Observe that the robot opens up the **Get List of items to purchase** sub-page and begins from its **Start** stage.

4. Now, let's fast forward to the **End** stage of the **Get List of items to purchase** page. Right-click on the **End** stage and select **Run to this stage**. The robot automatically moves from **Start** to the **Note** stage, and finally the **End** stage.

5. Press **Step** one more time. The robot exits the sub-page and takes you back to the **Main** page. The next stage, **Search and add item to cart**, is highlighted.

6. To speed things up, let's process the sub-page in a single step. Press **Step Over**
   . Instead of opening up the sub-page, the robot processed **Get List of items to purchase** in a single step and jumped straightaway to the next stage, **Send Email Notification**.

7. Press **Step** one more time to open up the **Send Email Notification** stage. Now, press **Step out**. The robot jumps out of the **Send Email Notification** page and back to the **Main** page.

As you can see, the step controls are very useful for controlling the robot as it works through the process. When you get more comfortable with the controls, you may favor use of the keyboard shortcuts over the buttons on the toolbar.

Join the Blue Prism community

Blue Prism has a portal that contains a wealth of knowledge about the product. Visit the site `https://portal.blueprism.com`. If you do not already have an account, simply click the **Sign Up here** link to get one.

The site is chock full of useful articles to solve almost every Blue Prism puzzle. There is also a community where you can post questions and get expert help from both the online community and the Blue Prism team. It is also the place to download the latest Blue Prism release and any VBO library files or add-ons. Throughout the book, we will reference material that is available on the website. So do sign up for an account if you have not already done so.

Summary

We covered the basics of building processes using Blue Prism. In this chapter, we rolled up our sleeves and created our very first process, complete with pages. We also took it for a test run to see the robot in action.

In the next chapter, we will flesh out the process and replace the stubs with the tasks that we actually want to execute.

3
Pages, Data Items, Blocks, Collections, and Loops

Earlier, we built the skeletal structure of our little purchasing process and then we took a sneak peek at what was inside the toolbox.

In this chapter, we will deep dive into the art of building processes with Blue Prism. The main objective is to explore most of the stage types available in the toolbox and to use them to add more details to the purchasing process that we have created earlier. We will start by taking a close look at the following stage types:

- **Pages**: Help us to organize the workflow into containers
- **Data Items**: The unit for storing data, such as text strings, and numbers
- **Blocks**: Groups stages or data items together
- **Collections**: Stores lists and tables
- **Loops**: Gets the process to repeat the same steps a fixed number of times

Taking a closer look at the toolbox

Open up the process that we executed earlier in Process Studio. Take a close look at the toolbox on the left-hand side. The items in the toolbox are called Stage types. These are the basic building blocks that make up all Blue Prism processes:

Stage Type	Description
Pointer	Changes the mouse to a pointer that can be used to select stages on the canvas to move, expand, or delete them
Link	Changes the mouse to enable linking between stages
Block	Creates a block for grouping stages or data items
Process	Adds a sub process to the process flow
Page	Adds a page (either new or existing) to the process flow
Action	Adds a business object action
Decision	A decision diamond for splitting the flow based on an evaluation criteria

Choice	A multi-decision tree that splits the flow into multiple paths based on a specified criteria
Calculation	A formula to update and store values back to a data item
Multi Calc	Multiple formulas to update and store values back to data items
Data Item	A container for storing a single value
Collection	A container for storing lists
Loop	A means to iterate through items in a collection
Note	Allows us to add remarks within the process flow
Anchor	Helps to keep the page organized and tidy by creating intermediate connection points
End	Specifies the end of the flow or page
Alert	Sends an alert to the process controllers
Exception	Used for exception handling
Recover	Used for exception handling
Resume	Used for exception handling

Pages

The first stage type that we used in our process is **page**. Theoretically, we could build the entire process within the **Main** page. However, as you can imagine, as the process grows in complexity and length, putting everything on a single page is going to be messy.

Think of pages as cabinet compartments that help us to organize the process into smaller parts. Imagine if you stuffed all your clothes into a single compartment in your wardrobe. It's going to take some time to get what you need when everything collapses into a pile of clothes. If you had separate drawers for shirts, another for pants, and perhaps more for socks and towels, if you ever needed to quickly grab a change of clothes, you will likely be able to find it much quicker.

The same thing can be said of pages. In our example, we have organized the process into three sub-pages:

- **Get List of Items to Purchase**
- **Search and Add Item to Basket**
- **Send Email Notification**

We then use the main page to link all the sub-pages together. In this way, we are able to see the outline of the process clearly from the main page. The details behind each step is hidden in the sub-page.

Inputs and outputs

Pages can pass information to each other. The information that is produced by, for example, Page 1 can be passed to Page 2 for further processing. They use outputs and inputs to communicate with one another.

In our process, the **Get List of items to purchase** page will retrieve the items to purchase. When it successfully gets the list, it puts this information in its output, as shown in the following diagram:

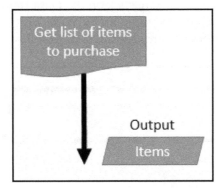

The next page, **Search and Add Item to Basket**, receives the list as an input, as shown in the following diagram:

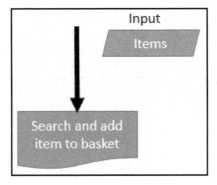

Adding outputs to a page

Let's configure the **Get List of items to purchase** page to place the collection that contains the list of items in its output:

1. Open the process that we created earlier. Edit the **Get List of items to purchase** page.
2. Double-click on the **End** stage. The **End Properties** dialog appears.
3. Click **Add**. A new row appears in the **Outputs** list. Enter the following values:
   - **Name**: Output - List of Items to Purchase
   - **Description**: Output collection that stores the list of items to purchase
   - **Data Type**: Collection
4. In the **Get Value from** column, click on the **Data Item** button 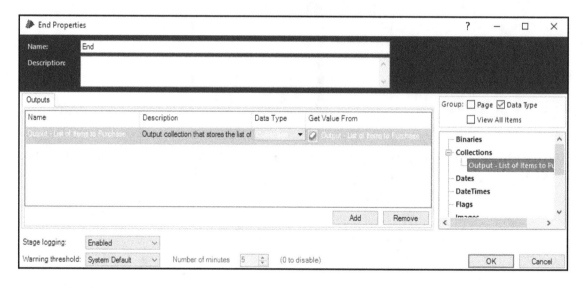. This will automatically create a collection with the name **Output - List of Items to Purchase**. The completed form should look as follows:

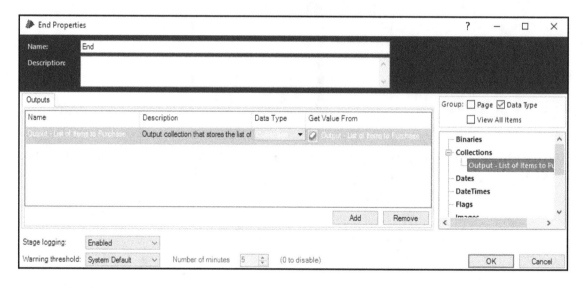

5. When you are ready, click the **OK** button to close the dialog. Take a look at the canvas. A new collection with the name **Output - List of Items to Purchase** has been added. Right now, the collection is empty. Later on, we will fill it with items:

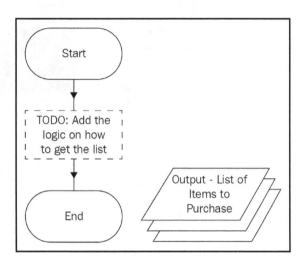

Adding inputs to a page

Let's move on to prepare the **Search and Add Item to Cart** page to receive the list of items to purchase.

1. Open the **Search and Add Item to Cart** page.
2. Double-click on the **Start** stage. The **Start properties** dialog opens.
3. Click **Add**. A new row appears in the **Inputs** list. Enter the following values:
   - **Name:** Input - List of Items to Purchase
   - **Description:** Input collection that stores the list of items to purchase
   - **Data Type:** Collection

4. In the **Get Value from** column, click on the **Data Item** button 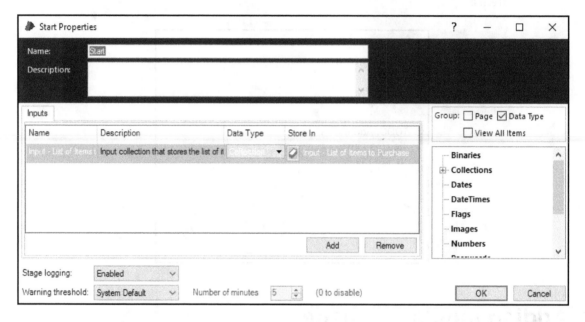. This will automatically create a collection with the name **Input - List of Items to Purchase**. The completed form should look as follows:

5. Click **OK** to close the **Start Properties** dialog. As before, the **Input - List of Items to Purchase** collection has been added to the canvas.

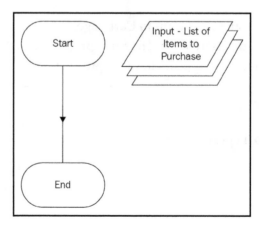

Passing information from page to page

Now that we have the outputs and inputs defined, let's get the process to pass the **List of Items to Purchase** collection from the **Get List of items to purchase** page to the **Search and Add Item to Cart** page.

At this point, the two pages are ready to deliver and receive the items, but they are still not talking to one another. We will connect them from the **Main** Page.

1. Go back to the **Main** page.
2. Double-click on the **Get List of items to purchase** page. This opens the **Page Reference Properties** dialog.
3. Click on the **Outputs** tab. Notice that the output that we just defined for the page is listed.
4. The **Store In** field tells Blue Prism where to store the output collection to. Enter **List of Items to Purchase** as the name of the collection. As we have yet to create it, click on the **Data Item** icon ☑ to automatically create a new collection of the same name:

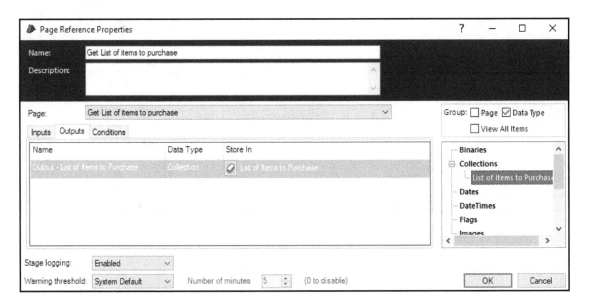

5. Click **OK** to close the **Page Reference Properties** dialog. The **Get List of items to purchase** page now passes the **List of Items to Purchase** collection back to the **Main** page.

6. We will now proceed to pass that collection as an input to the **Search and Add Item to Cart** page. From the **Main** page, double-click on the **Search and Add Item to Cart** page. The **Page Reference Properties** dialog opens.

7. Take a look at the **Inputs** tab. The **Input - List of Items to Purchase** field that we have defined previously appears in the listing. Drag and drop the **List of Items to Purchase** collection from the right-hand panel to the value field. The completed dialog appears as shown in the following screenshot:

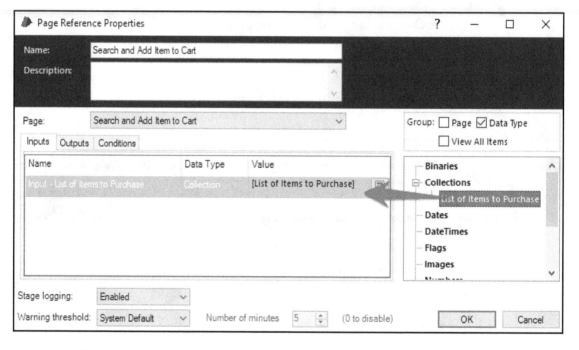

8. Click **OK** to close the dialog.

Now, the **Search and Add Item to Cart** page will receive the **Items to Purchase** collection.

Data items

Do you remember algebra from math lessons in school? We used variables to represent a number that we needed to solve, as follows:

```
X = 10

Y = 8

Z = X + Y
```

Later on, we learned how to solve for Z, which, in our little example, equals 18.

Data items are the X and Y variables of Blue Prism. They are used to contain value items in our process that are used for expressions, decisions, and calculations, including the number of items to purchase, the email address of the purchaser, and the website address.

They can contain anything from text to numbers to dates. Blue Prism recognizes the following types of data items:

Data type	Description
Date	Stores a date
DateTime	Stores a date with a time value
Number	Can be a whole number, or a decimal, positive, or negative number. Also used for storing dollar values
Password	A masked text that appears as a series of dots when you look at it. As the name suggests, it is typically used to store passwords retrieved from Blue Prism's credential manager
Text	Stores strings
Time	Stores a time value
TimeSpan	Stores a length of time
Image	Stores an image
Binary	Stores binary data, for example, a file

Adding a data item

Let's add the path to the Excel file that contains the list of all the items to purchase as a data item. In later chapters of the book, we will instruct the robot to use this path value to open up the Excel:

1. Open the **Get List of items to purchase** page.
2. Drag and drop a data item from the toolbox to the canvas.

3. Double-click on the newly added data item. The **Data Properties** dialog appears. Enter the following:

  - **Name:** Shopping List Excel File Path
  - **Data Type:** Text
  - **Initial Value:** c:\shopping\ShoppingList_Henry.xlsx

4. Click **OK** to close the dialog. The data item appears on the canvas as a parallelogram with its names and value inside:

Making a data item visible across pages

By default, data items are designed to be visible only from within the page where it is located. We just added a data item named **Shopping List Excel File Path**. We use it in the **Get List of items to purchase** page to read the contents of an Excel file (we have not actually done that yet, but we will do so later in the book). If we need to get the path to the Excel file in another page, say **Search and Add Item to Cart**, we won't be able to do so.

For data items to be seen across pages (also known as global data items), we need to set their visibility property. Let's make the **Shopping List Excel File Path Data** item a global one.

  - Double-click on the **Shopping List Excel File Path** data item to open up the properties dialog.
  - Uncheck the **Visibility** checkbox. Click **OK** to close the dialog.

The **Shopping List Excel File Path** data item can now be used by any page within the process.

When do we use inputs/outputs versus global data items?

Both inputs/outputs and global data items pass information from one page to another. Both appear to do the same thing of passing information around, so which one do you use and when? You can choose to define all shared data items as global. Or you may pass them around as inputs/outputs. It is for this reason that Globals tend to be misused—when you have too many global data items, it becomes cumbersome to keep track of where they are used and what they are used for. Therefore, as a rule of thumb, only make a data item global when it really makes sense to do so.

Blocks

Just as we used pages to organize a large process into mini routines, blocks may be used to group data items of the same type together. When you were adding inputs and outputs to both pages and action stages, Blue Prism automatically created the data items and placed them on the canvas. As we build the process, the data items will be scattered all over the page, making it very hard to look for them.

As a best practice, we organize the data items using blocks. It does not change the behavior of the process or alter it in any way. The blocks merely add visual appeal to the process diagram, making it easier to read and maintain.

Common categories for grouping data items include the following:

- **Inputs**: Places all inputs to the page in one block
- **Outputs**: Places all outputs to the page in one block
- **Locals**: Places the remaining data items used only within the page in one block
- **Globals**: Places data items that are shared across all pages in a single block, usually on the main page

Blocks are also used to group stages that share the same exception routine. We will learn more about this technique later in the book.

Let's organize the data items on our pages:

- Open the **Search and Add Item to Cart** page.
- Click on the **Block** stage type on the toolbox.
- Click and drag on the canvas to draw a box that is big enough to fit the data items on the page. By default, the block is named **Block1**.
- Double-click on the little white box that displays the name **Block1** (Note: you can't double-click anywhere else, you must click on the name). The **Block Properties** dialog appears. Use it to change the name of the block to **Inputs**.
- Click **OK** to close the dialog. We want to move the data items into the block.

  Before we do so, click on the pointer in the toolbox to switch back the mouse.
- Drag and drop the **Inputs - List of Items to Purchase** collection into the block, as shown in the following diagram:

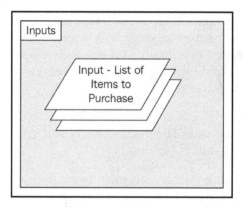

Throughout the book, we will continue to group our data items into blocks. Just like having a desktop that is neat and tidy, it makes for a much more pleasant and mess-free coding experience.

Collections

Collections are good for storing all sorts of lists. It is a special type of data item within Blue Prism that has the capacity to store multiple rows of data in a single table.

Typical types of lists that we may want the robot to work with include an entire Excel worksheet or a database table. As long as there are rows of data, the robot can be trained to read them and store the list in a collection.

Defining a collection

Earlier, in the **Get List of items to purchase** page, we created a blank collection named **Output - List of Items to Purchase**. It didn't contain any headers or rows. Let's proceed to define a table that looks as follows:

Item name
Low carb granola cereal
Cap'N Crunch breakfast cereal

1. Open the **Get List of items to purchase** page.
2. Double-click on the **Output – List of Items to Purchase** collection. The **Collection Properties** dialog opens.
3. We are now going to add the column to our collection. Within the **Collection Properties** dialog, click **Add Field**. Within the **Fields** tab, a new row is added. Enter the following:
    - **Name:** Item Name
    - **Type:** Text
    - **Description:** The name of the item to purchase
4. Click the **Initial Values** tab. Our list is currently empty since we have not added anything to it yet. Go ahead and click on **Add Row**. A new row appears and is ready for you to fill in the data. Add some items to purchase alongside requester names, like the ones shown here.

Later on in the book, we will train the robot to actually get the list of items to purchase from an Excel spreadsheet. For now, we will just enter the values directly into the collection, as demonstrated in the following collection:

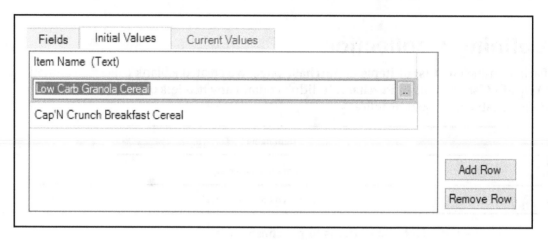

5. We are done. Click **OK** to close the **Collection Properties** dialog. When you do so, take a look at the collection on the canvas. Because we have added two items to the list, it says Row 1 of 2 beneath the name (You may have to expand the visual size of the collection to see the full text):

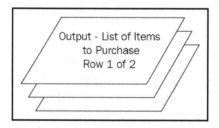

Loops

We use collections to store rows of data. We then use loops to go through each row one by one and process it. Here's an example of a loop:

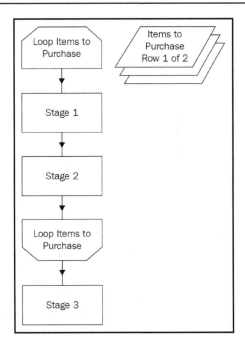

A loop always starts by looking at a specific collection; let's say, for example, the **Items to Purchase** collection. At the start of the loop, we read the first row, which, in our example, is the low carb granola cereal. The robot proceeds to process the low carb granola cereal by running **Stage 1**, followed by **Stage 2**. When the robot completes its processing of **Stage 2**, it will check whether there are more rows in the collection that has not been processed. If there are, it will automatically loop back to **Stage 1**. Otherwise, it will proceed to **Stage 3**.

Adding a loop

Now we have created the collection to store the list of items to purchase. In this next step, we will get the robot to look at each item and attempt to *purchase* it:

1. Open the **Search and Add Item to Cart** page.

2. Earlier, we simply linked the **Start** to the **End** stage. As we will be inserting additional steps in our process, we will need to delete this link. Click on the arrow head and press the **Delete** key:

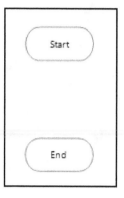

3. Drag a **Loop** stage from the toolbox and drop it onto the canvas directly beneath the **Start** stage. Note that the loop always comes as a pair – it will have a **Loop Start** as well as a **Loop End:**

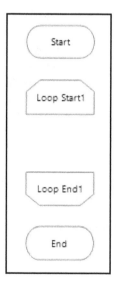

4. Double-click on the **Loop Start** stage (note: not the **Loop End** stage). In the **Loop Properties** dialog, give the loop a name. A common practice is to insert the name of the collection that you are looping. This makes it visually very easy to see which collection the loop is working with. Here, we enter **Loop Input - List of Items to Purchase**.

5. In the **Collection** field, choose **Input – List of Items to Purchase** from the drop-down list. The completed dialog appears as follows:

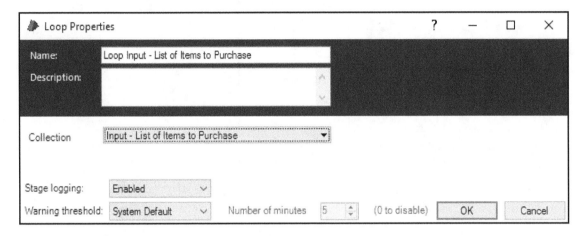

6. Click **OK** to close the dialog. Back on the canvas, the loop appears as follows:

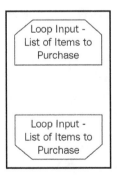

7. We will simulate the purchase of the items by adding a **Note** stage. Drag and drop a **Note** stage between the **Loop Start** and **Loop End** stages. Set the note text to **Search and add the item to the cart**. We will be building the full instructions as we progress through the book. For now, we will use this note as a placeholder for this action.

---

8. Finally, link the stages together so that the diagram appears as follows:

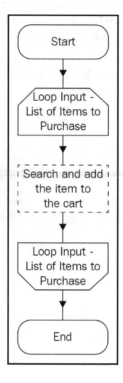

Reset the process and run it again. Observe how the robot moves through the loop twice – once for each item in the collection.

When defining a loop, one of the common mistakes that developers make is not handling errors that occur within the loop. Let's say, if there are 10 items in the collection, should there be an error processing item number 3 out of 10, the process will terminate immediately, leaving item numbers 4-10 unprocessed.

As a best practice, always have exception handling within the loop, such that if there is an error in processing, say item number 3, the process will take note of the exception and proceed onto item number 4.

We will cover Exception Handling in more detail, together with the exact instructions to manage the error in this loop, in later chapters.

Checking for errors using the validation tool

We have completed building a draft of our process. Have we made any errors? Blue Prism is shipped with a validation tool to help us look for any configuration errors that we may have unwittingly made. Well, it's not going to go through your code to check to see whether the Robot bought the correct products or emailed the correct people. It's more like the spelling and grammar check tool in Microsoft Word. Instead of spelling and grammar checks, the validation tool looks for configuration errors in our process, such as:

- Stages that are not linked to anything
- Missing data items
- Missing business objects
- Missing links
- Missing pages

Let's see if there are any configuration errors with the process so far:

1. First, let's generate an error. Go to the **Email Notification Page**. Delete the link between the **Start** and **End** stage.
2. From the toolbar, look for the **Validate** button. Next to the button is a number that indicates the error count that Blue Prism has detected so far. It appears as if we have one error to correct:

3. Click the **Validate** button. The **Process Validation** dialog opens. All the errors and advice (or warnings) are listed. Blue Prism has detected that the **Send Email Notification** page is missing a link:

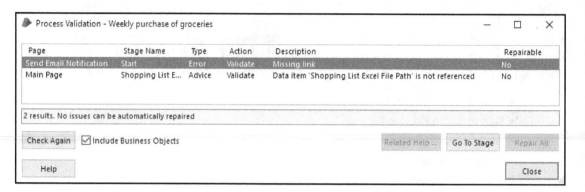

Page	Stage Name	Type	Action	Description	Repairable
Send Email Notification	Start	Error	Validate	Missing link	No
Main Page	Shopping List E...	Advice	Validate	Data item 'Shopping List Excel File Path' is not referenced	No

2 results. No issues can be automatically repaired

Check Again ☑ Include Business Objects   Related Help ...   Go To Stage   Repair All

Help   Close

4. Click **Go To Stage** to zoom into the problem area. Blue Prism automatically brings you to the correct page and highlights the erroneous stage in yellow, as demonstrated in the following diagram:

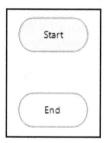

5. Link back the **Start** to the **End** to correct the error. Click on the **Validate** button again. Notice that the error count is now 0. The error no longer shows up in the list of errors and warnings.

The tool is still complaining that the **Shopping List Excel File Path** data item is created but not used anywhere in the page. That's because we have not finished building the process. For now, we shall ignore that warning.

Summary

In this chapter, we saw how pages are used to compartmentalize the logic of the process so that it can be broken down into smaller and maintainable units. We added inputs and outputs and saw how to pass information from page to page.

Next, we took a look at data items and observed how they are used to store all kinds of information that is used in a process. If we needed to store multiple rows of data, we use a collection instead of a single data item.

We also studied the all-important concept of loops. Robots were built to perform repeatable tasks, and loops are right in the centre of the action, getting robots to perform the same set of instructions over and over again.

Finally, we used the built-in validation tool to help check for any syntax errors that may have crept into the process.

In the next chapter, we will look at the remaining stage types used in processes, namely, actions, decisions, choices, and calculations.

4
Actions, Decisions, Choices, and Calculations

In this chapter, we will continue to build up the purchasing process. While we are at it, we will explore the remaining stages in the toolbox, namely the following:

- **Actions**: Behaves as the *arms* of the robot. It will do things such as click on buttons or press the keyboard.
- **Decisions**: Enables the robot to choose which path to take based on a given algorithm.
- **Choices**: Helps the robot through a series of decisions.
- **Calculations**: Builds formulas and expressions to determine the value of something

These are the stages where we are able to teach the robot to *think* somewhat. These stages are absolutely critical when building any process. Without them, we won't be able to build meaningful processes at all.

Actions

Blue Prism ships with a ready-to-use set of libraries that integrate with a myriad of applications and common functions that greatly speed up development time. There are two types of libraries: Internal business objects, and visual business objects.

Internal business objects are at the core of Blue Prism. They are built within the Blue Prism application. Some of the commonly used internal business objects are as follows:

- **Collections**: Adds rows, copies rows, counts columns, counts rows, removes all rows, and removes a single row
- **Calendar**: Provides actions for getting working days and public holidays from the internally maintained Blue Prism calendar
- **Work Queues**: Various actions for work queues that we will discuss later in the book.
- **Credentials**: Getting and setting passwords stored within Blue Prism. Used by the robot to access various applications.

Visual business objects are extensions that have been developed either by Blue Prism or third-party vendors, or even yourself. They require a release manager to upload to Blue Prism before they can be used by developers. They are visual because these extensions usually (but not always) work with external applications, such as Microsoft Excel, Outlook, Word, and even Internet Explorer. Some extensions are utilities that provide easier manipulation of data, such as strings, dates, and numbers.

It is through this comprehensive set of libraries that Blue Prism is able to achieve so much automation with minimal build time. In the next chapter, we will learn how to build our own visual business object. For now, let's try out the ones that have already been installed. We will try out the **Collections** internal business object.

Adding an action to count the number of rows in a collection

Let's use the internal business object for **Collections** to count the number of items in our **List of Items to Purchase** collection. We will need the item count later when we are checking to see whether the list is empty (we won't need to purchase anything if there are no orders). Let's continue editing the **Weekly purchase of groceries** process that we started in the previous chapters:

1. Open the **Weekly purchase of groceries** process and edit the **Search and Add Item to Cart** page.
2. Delete the link between the **Start** stage and the **Loop Start** stage, shown as follows:

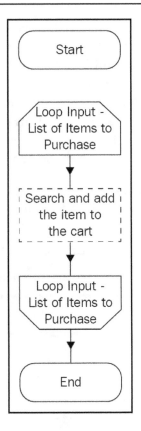

3. Drag and drop an **Action** from the toolbox to the canvas. Drop it directly beneath the **Start** stage as such:

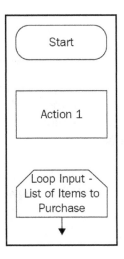

4. Double-click on the newly added **Action** stage. The **Action properties** dialog opens.

5. In the **Name** field, enter: **Count the number of items to purchase.**

6. In the **Business Object** dropdown, scroll all the way to the bottom until you see the section **Internal Business Objects**. Choose **Collections**.

7. In the **Action** dropdown, choose **Count Rows**.

8. Now, we will specify the collection whose rows we want to count. In the **Inputs** section, enter the name of the collection. Here, the action is expecting the name **Text**. Enter `Input - List of Items to Purchase`. Note that because it is expecting **Text**, the opening and closing double quotes are important, so remember to type those in as well. The following screenshot shows the completed dialog:

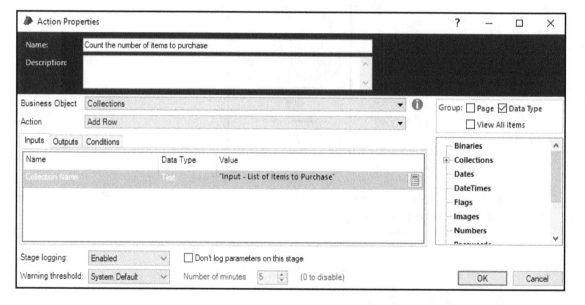

9. Click on **Outputs**. The action already has **Count** listed in the Outputs section. That contains the number value of the number of rows in the collection. All you need to do is to tell Blue Prism the name of the data item that should store it.

10. In the **Store In** field, enter **Number of Items to Purchase** (note: no double quotes!). We have yet to create this data item, so go ahead and click on the **Data Item** icon for Blue Prism to automatically generate it. The data item appears in Data Explorer as soon as its created, as shown in the following screenshot:

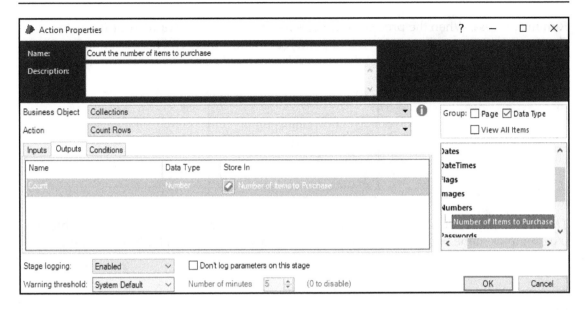

11. Click the **OK** button to close the dialog.
12. To finish off, link the stages. Here is how the completed diagram appears:

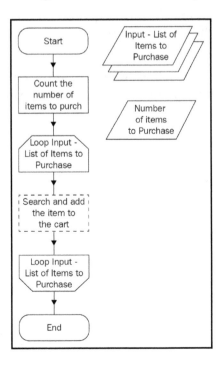

Run the process. When the process completes its run, look at the **Number of Items to Purchase** data item (you may have to expand it to make it bigger). There is a number 2 below its name, which means that the process has correctly counted the two rows that we have added to the collection:

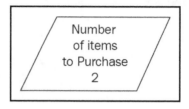

There are many more actions that we can use to build up our process. As we work through the examples in the book, we will encounter more actions and even build some of them ourselves.

Decisions

As we plot the workflow on the canvas, there are times when we need the robot to make a decision. Within the decision, there is always a question. Unlike the open-ended questions that confound philosophers, the kind of questions that our robots deal with always result in a Yes or No answer.

For example, is the weather hot? If yes, eat some ice-cream. Otherwise (no, it's cold), drink hot chocolate. In the world of programming, a decision stage models an if-else statement.

In a typical workflow diagram, we draw this out using a decision diamond as shown here:

Adding a decision to decide whether to proceed to purchase the items

Let's add decision logic to our purchasing process. After counting the number of items, if we find that the list is empty, we will decide not to proceed with the routine to add the items to the cart:

1. Open the **Search and Add Item to Cart** page.

2. Delete the link between the **Count the number of items to purchase** and the **Loop Start** stage, as shown in the following diagram:

3. Drag a **Decision** stage and drop it just above the **Loop Start** stage (refer to the following diagram):

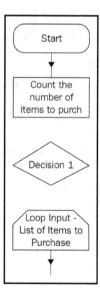

4. Double-click on the newly added **Decision** stage. The **Decision Properties** dialog appears. Take a look at two key areas in this dialog:

   - **Name** of the stage. For decisions, we usually phrase the name in the form of a question. For this example, enter: Is the list empty?

   - **Expression,** which is expecting a formula to derive the answer to the question. Here, we will enter the expression that will be computed by the robot to see whether the list is empty. Don't worry about what to type in here; we will take you through the steps in the next exercise. For now, leave it blank.

5. Click **OK** to close the dialog.

6. We have configured the decision stage. Now, let's link it up to the rest of the page. Link the **Count the number of items to purchase** stage to the **Is the list empty?** decision, as follows:

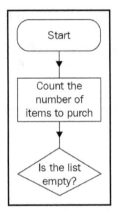

7. Drag an **End** stage and drop it next to the decision, as shown here:

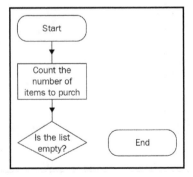

8. Link the **Is the list empty?** stage to the **End** stage, as shown in the following diagram. Take note of the **Yes** that appears next to the arrow. What this means is that when **Is the basket empty?** is **Yes**, the process will flow to the **End** stage:

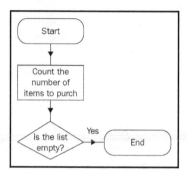

9. Link the **Is the list empty?** stage to the **Loop Start** stage. This time, the text above the arrow is **No**. When the list of items to purchase is not empty (we have orders in the list!), it means that we have something to buy and we will trigger the part of the process that will perform the task. At this point, the diagram should appear as follows:

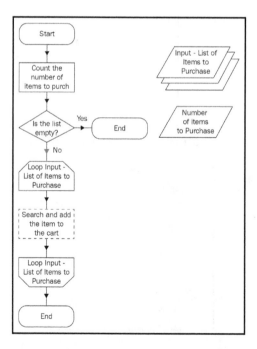

Building an expression

The diagram looks complete. However, recall that we have not filled in the expression for the **Is the list empty?** stage. Right now, it's just an empty question. Without an expression, the robot will not be able to understand what an empty list means. What we will do in this section is to build the expression to indicate whether or not the list is empty.

The list will be considered empty when the **Number of Items to Purchase** is equal to 0. As long as there is at least one item in the list, we will need to purchase it. Alright, let's get to it.

1. Double-click on the **Is the list empty?** stage to open up the properties dialog. Take a look at the bottom half of the dialog, as shown in the following screenshot.
   The Expression Builder is divided into three areas:

   - At the top, there is the **Expression** itself. You can either choose to key in the expression or use the expression builder tools to generate it.
   - On the left, you see the **Functions**. There are many built-in functions that we can use to perform calculations. It's very similar to the formulas that we are familiar with in Excel.
   - To the right is the **Data Explorer**. You are presented with the list of data items that we have declared within the process.

   The nice thing about Blue Prism is that it gives us the convenience of dragging and dropping items to build up a formula instead of keying it in. Let's use it to generate the expression to decide whether or not the list of items to purchase is empty.

To do so, we will check to see whether the **Number of Items to Purchase** equals 0:

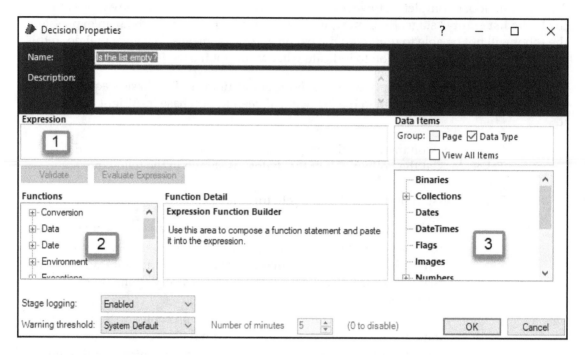

2. From the **Functions** list, expand **Logic**. Click on the **Equal (=)** function. Notice that the **Function Detail** section is updated with a description of the function, along with the inputs. It says that the Equal function gets a flag saying whether one value is equal to another; for example, 5 = 3 + 2 results in True. In addition, there are two operands:
   - Operand A (what appears to the left of the equal sign)
   - Operand B (what appears to the right of the equal sign)

Personally, I find this particular feature very useful. There are just too many functions to remember by heart. Having the builder means we don't have to memorize everything and also ensures that we don't make any careless typo mistakes. Here's how the dialog looks like when the **Equal** function is selected.

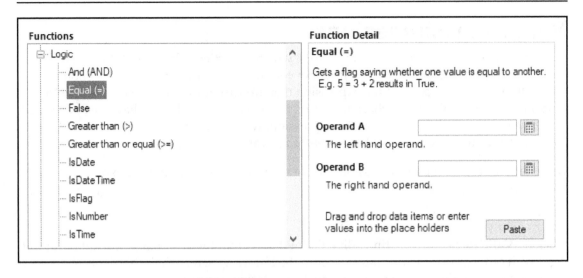

3. All we need to do now is to fill in what should go into Operand A and Operand B.

4. Let's fill in Operand A first. From **Data Explorer**, expand **Numbers**. Drag and drop **Number of Items to Purchase** into **Operand A**.

5. Next, in **Operand B**, enter the number 0.

6. Finally, click **Paste**. The following expression is generated:

Notice that the data item has square brackets surrounding it. You will see many more examples of expressions as we build up the process.

Underneath the expression are two buttons: **Validate** and **Evaluate Expression**. Let's take a look at what they are.

Validating expressions

The **Validate** button checks for syntax errors, which is particularly helpful if you have hand-typed the expression yourself. It works very much like the spellcheck function in Word. If there are any parts of the expression that are structurally incorrect, it will help to detect it. Click on **Validate** to check for errors in the expression that we have just generated. Since we used the builder to create the expression, we are not expecting any errors. Blue Prism gives a prompt that says **The expression is valid**.

Now, let's try to fake a bad expression. Delete the number **0,** such that the expression reads as follows:

```
[Number of Items to Purchase] =
```

Click on **Validate** again. This time, Blue Prism detects that there is something not quite right with our expression and states (refer to the following screenshot) that "The '=' operator requires an expression on the right—no such expression found":

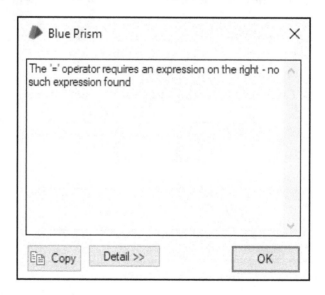

Put back the number 0 to correct the error in the expression.

Evaluating expressions

The **Evaluate Expression** button gives you a chance to run the expression with test values so that you can see whether it works. It is very useful when building complicated expressions, since we can check to see whether there are any logic errors in the expression before embedding it in the process.

Let's try it out to see how it works:

1. Click **Evaluate Expression**. The **Expression Test Wizard** opens.
2. Set the **Number of Items to Purchase** to 0.
3. Click **Test**. Notice that the result is **True**, which means that the expression will evaluate to an empty list if the **Number of Items to Purchase** is 0.
4. Now, repeat the test again. This time, however, set the **Number of Items to Purchase** to 1. Notice that the result is now False, which means that the list is not empty.
5. Continue to test the expression with more temporary values. When you are done, click **Close** to exit the wizard.

Now that we have validated and tested the expression, let's get back to the rest of the process. Click **OK** to close the **Decision Properties** dialog.

Choices

A choice stage is very similar to a decision. Previously, we saw that a decision asks a single question, for example: Is the weather hot? It always results in a yes-no type of answer. A choice is made up of multiple decisions which gives us the ability to program for more than one decision point. We can use it to create a more complicated scenario, such as the following:

- If the **temperature is ≥ 30 °C**, we will eat ice cream
- If the **temperature is < 30 °C and ≥ 25 °C**, we will drink cooled water
- Otherwise, if the **temperature is < 25°C**, we will drink hot chocolate

In a flowchart diagram, the preceding logic will appear as shown in the following diagram. Note that it is made up of many decision diamonds:

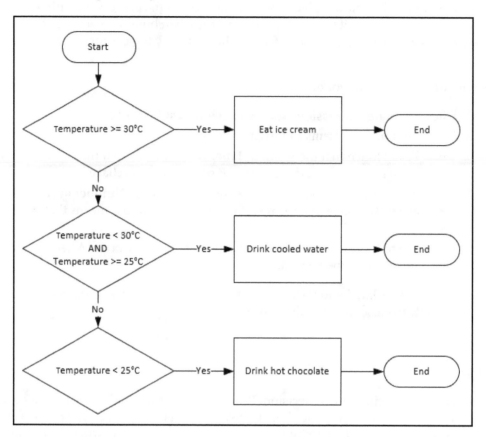

Using a choice to determine the email address of the requester

When we defined the collection, **List of Items to Purchase**, earlier, we supplied the name of the item as well as the requester's name. Given the name of the requester, we want to get their email address so that we can notify them at the end of the process whether or not the item was successfully purchased.

We may have a look-up table that matches the name of the person to their email address:

Name	Email address
Henry	henry@somewhere.com
Peter	peter@somewhere.com
Margaret	margaret@somewhere.come
Otherwise	admin@somewhere.com

Let's program this logic to perform this matching to the process using a **Choice** stage.

1. Open the **Send Email Notification** sub-page. Delete the arrow that links the **Start** to the **End** stage.
2. Add a **Data Item** to the page. Give it the following property values:
   - **Name:** Requester
   - **Data type:** Text
3. Add another data item to the page. Give it the following property values:
   - **Name:** Email address
   - **Data Type:** Text
4. Drag a **Choice** stage from the canvas and drop it beneath the **Start** stage. Two diamonds are automatically drawn on the screen (refer to the following diagram). The first is called **Choice 1,** and the second is **Otherwise1**:

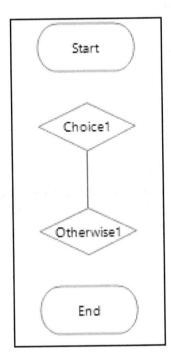

5. Double-click on **Choice1**. This brings up the **Choice Property** dialog. Rename the stage to **Get Email Address of Requester**.

   Now, take a close look at the **Choice Properties** dialog. It consists of a table with two columns:

   - **Choice Name** is a label that helps us to describe what the question is.
   - **Choice Criterion** is the expression that will be used to evaluate whether or not the conditions for the decision have been fulfilled.

6. Right now, the choice table is empty. Click **Add** three times to insert three new rows. Fill it up with the following values:

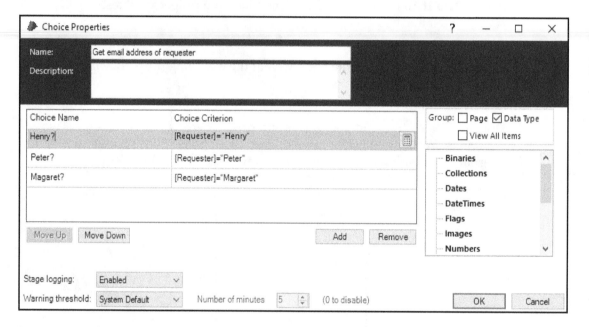

 You can either choose to type in the expression by hand or you can click on the calculator to bring up the **Expression Editor** and build it visually. It's entirely up to you to decide how you want to enter it.

Click **OK** to close the dialog. Back in the flowchart diagram, notice that three little diamonds have been added between the bigger diamonds. Each little diamond represents a choice in the list of choices. We added three choices earlier, so therefore there are now three little diamonds, as shown here:

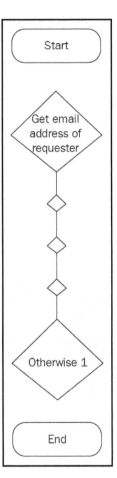

7. Add four **Calculation** stages to the canvas. Place each calculation stage next to the little diamonds. Add one more next to **Otherwise1,** as shown here:

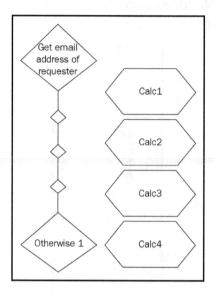

8. Use the **Link** tool to link each little diamond to the calculation stage next to it. As you link it up, you can see the labels that we used to describe the choice appear, as demonstrated in the following diagram:

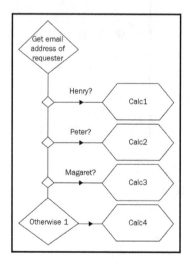

9. We will discuss more about the calculation stage in just a moment. Meanwhile, double-click **Calc1** and configure it as follows:

- **Name**: Set Email Address
- **Expression**: "henry@somewhere.com" (don't forget the double quotes!)
- **Store Result in**: Email Address (drag and drop from **Data Explorer**):

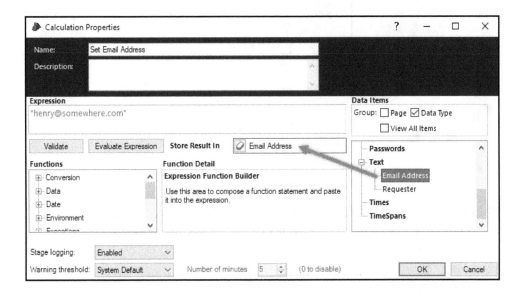

10. Repeat this step to fill in the **Calc2, Calc3,** and **Calc4** stages for Peter, Margaret, and the administrator (the administrator will be the email address for the "Otherwise" case) as well.

11. Use the anchor stage to lay out the links neatly, as shown here:

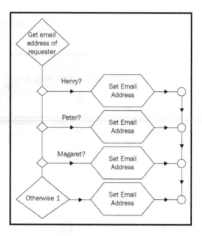

12. Finally, link the **Start** stage to the **Get email address of requester** stage, and the calculation stage from **Otherwise1** to **End**. The completed diagram is shown here:

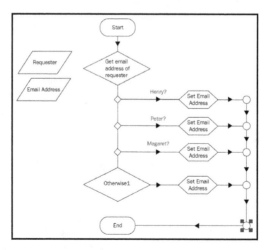

Save the process and give it a test run. In the **Requester** data item, insert **Henry**, for example, as the initial value. Watch the robot move through the **Henry?** path and set the email address to `henry@somewhere.com`. Repeat the test for the other email addresses and see the choice stage at work.

Calculations

We had a sneak peek into calculations when we were exploring choices. Let's take a more in-depth look at it in this section. We are familiar with mathematical calculations, like the following example that we saw when we studied data items:

```
X = 10

Y = 8

Z = X + Y
```

What is the value of Z? While we can manually whip out a calculator and compute that $Z = 10 + 8 = 18$, robots use the calculation stage to apply these formulas to get the answer:

 We can do a lot more than calculate numbers. In the next example, we will use the Calculate stage to prepare an email message for the requester of the item to let him know that the item has been added to the cart.

Calculating the email notification message

Follow these steps to compose an email message to be sent by the robot when it completes adding items to the cart. We will prepare an email template that contains the following text:

```
Hi <Requestor>
I have completed adding your items to the cart.

regards
Robot
```

The calculation will replace the `<Requestor>`, text, with the actual name of the person making the purchase, for example, `Henry`. This gives the email a more personal touch:

1. Open the **Send Email Notification** page.
2. Drag a **Data Item** from the toolbox to the page. Give it the following property values:
   - **Name**: Email Template
   - **Data type**: Text
3. In the **Initial Value** field, enter the text for the email template, as shown in the following screenshot. You may click on the double dots ⬚ at the end of the field to open the multi-line editor:

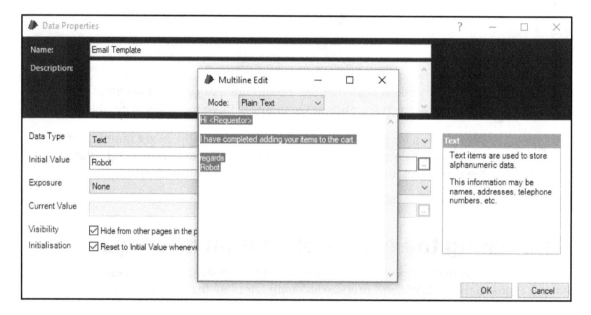

4. Add another data item. Configure it as follows:
   - **Name**: Email Message
   - **Data type**: Text
5. Delete the link between the **Start** and **Get email address of requester** stages.
6. Drag a **Calculation** stage and drop it directly beneath the **Start** stage. Double-click on the newly added calculation stage to edit its properties. Name the stage **Prepare Email**:

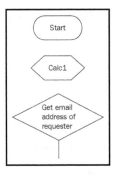

7. Now, let's work on building the expression. First, in the **Functions** list, choose
    Text | Replace. Take a look at the **Function Detail** section. It expects three
    inputs: **Text, Pattern,** and **NewText**:

    - **Text** is looking for the original text that we want to work with. We
      have that defined in **Email Template**. Drag and drop **Email Template**
      from **Data Explorer** to **Text**.

    - The **Pattern** field is the string that we are looking for in the text that we
      want to replace. In this example, the pattern is the string
      "<Requester>". Go ahead and key it in. Remember the double quotes
      as you do so.

    - **NewText** tells the robot what to replace the pattern string with. In this
      example, we want to replace it with the actual name of the requester.
      Drag **Requester** from Data Explorer and drop it into the **NewText**
      field. The completed function is shown in the following screenshot:

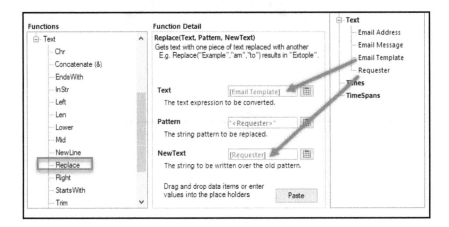

8. When you are ready, click **Paste**. See the expression that is generated in the **Expression** box:

> **Expression**
> Replace([Email Template], "<Requester>", [Requester])

9. We want to store the output of this expression so that we can use it in our process later. Let's store it in **Email Message**. To do so, drag **Email Message** from **Data Explorer** and drop it into the **Store Result In** field. This is what the completed dialog looks like:

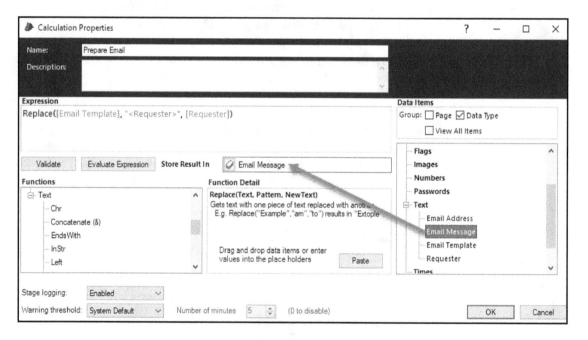

10. Click **OK** to close the **Calculation Properties** dialog. Back on the canvas, link all the stages together. The completed diagram should look as follows:

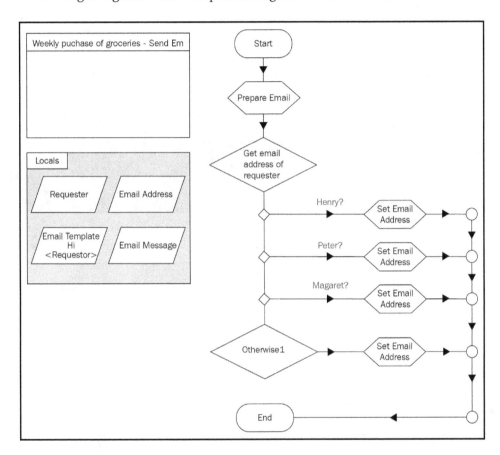

Give the page a test run by setting different names in the **Requester** data item. Observe the changes in **Email Message** as you set different names.

Multi calc

The multi calc stage works in the same way as the calculation stage, except that it can store multiple calculations. If you look at the properties dialog of a multi calc, you can see a table that lists all the calculations to be performed.

In the following screenshot, we have two calculations in the list:

- A + B = C
- C + D = E

The robot will work through the first expression, and then the second expression. You can use the **Move Up** and **Move Down** buttons to change the order in which the lines are processed:

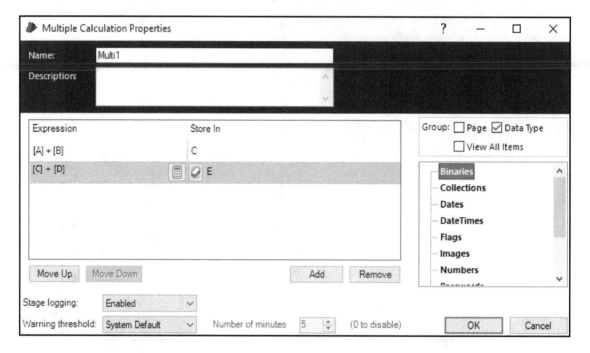

We could have split the stage into two single calculation stages and it would have worked the same way. However, if you have a set of complex calculation steps, putting them all into a multi calc will simplify the representation of the stage. You can perform the same number of calculations and take up only a fraction of the screen space.

Summary

In this chapter, we have completed the first draft of the purchasing process. In doing so, we used stages that are key building blocks of any process. We first learned how to use the built-in business objects within Blue Prism to perform actions, such as counting the number of rows in a collection. Next, we used the decision stage to teach the robot how to make small decisions that will always result in a yes-no answer. For more complicated decisions, such as matching the name to the email address of a person, we used the choices stage. Finally, we gave calculations a spin and used it to generate the email message that we will send back to the requester.

While it is cool to have ready-to-use business objects at our disposal, nothing beats having the flexibility to build your own and extend the functionality that Blue Prism provides out of the box. We will look at implementing our own business objects in the next chapter.

5
Implementing Business Objects

In our process, we are planning to train the robot to get the list of items, search and add items to the cart, and then send email notifications. So far, we've only added notes to the parts of the process that are supposed to perform these tasks. We have not actually taught the robot to click on any buttons or key in anything. That's because it is with business objects that all that action takes place.

In this chapter, we will discuss the following topics:

- What business objects are and how they are used
- We will familiarize ourselves with Business Studio
- We will then take you through step by step regarding how you can go about creating your own business objects by building our own Amazon website object
- Finally, we will see how to use the business object from the purchasing process that we have been building

What is a business object?

In Blue Prism, a business object is an object that models the applications that the robot interacts with. As we will see in a moment, we use business objects to do cool stuff such as the following:

- Opening and closing an application
- Writing into text boxes
- Reading messages on screen
- Clicking on links and submit buttons

The key reason for business objects to be a separate entity from processes is because business objects can be shared by multiple processes. In a real-world scenario, you are likely to have more than one process working with the same application. By way of example, let's say we build an Amazon business object. We are already planning to build a purchasing process that interacts with it. There could also be another process that uses the same Amazon business object to post comments or reviews about a product; or a process to track price changes throughout the year; or perhaps a process that constantly checks on competing products and their ranking on the sales board.

Creating a business object

Let's see business objects in action. First, we will start with creating our very own Business Object, **Amazon – Search**. We add -Search to the end of the name for the purpose of describing what we want to do with the object.

In the **Amazon – Search** object, we will empower the robot to perform these actions:

- **Launch**: Opens Internet Explorer and navigates to the page http://www.amazon.com
- **Terminate**: Closes the Internet Explorer browser

As we progress through the build, we will add more complex stuff, such as the **Search** and **Add to basket** actions:

1. Launch the Blue Prism interactive client. In the Studio tab, click on the **Objects** folder, the container that Blue Prism uses for storing all the Business Objects in the system. Notice that, like the **Processes** folder, the **Objects** folder has a **folder** named **Default** that was pre-created by the installer.
2. Right-click **Objects**. Choose **Create Object** from the menu.
3. Name the object **Amazon – Search**. Go ahead and key that into the **Name** field. Click **Next** when this is completed.

4. It's always a good idea to provide a brief write-up about what capabilities this object is going to provide. You can write anything you want to, but something along the lines of the following will suffice: **Launches the Amazon site and closes the browser**. After keying in the description, click **Finish**.

5. The newly created Business Object is created in the **Default** folder.

Organizing Business Objects into folders

As time goes by, you will most likely be adding more and more Business Objects and the list is going to get rather cluttered. Getting to the one you want to work with would require quite a bit of eyeballing and scrolling. Imagine trying to locate an object from a list of hundreds.

Just like processes, we can organize Business Objects into folders. Let's create a folder named **Amazon** and place our Business Object within it.

1. From Studio, right-click **Objects**. Choose **Create Group**.

2. A folder appears in the list, ready for you to key in its new name. Let's call the folder **Amazon**. Press **Enter** when you are done.

3. The folder is ready for use. Click on the **Amazon – Basic** object to select it, drag it into the **Amazon** folder, and then release the mouse to drop it there. The Amazon Business Object is successfully filed to the **Amazon** folder.

Taking a look at Business Studio

Now that the Business Object has been created, let's build it. Double-click on the newly created object to open it in Business Studio. It looks somewhat similar to Process Studio, but with a few differences (refer to the following screenshot):

1. There are new stages in the toolbar (we will get to what these are in a bit).

2. What were previously **Page** tabs are now **Action** tabs.

3. There is a new **Application Modeller** button in the toolbar, as demonstrated in the following screenshot:

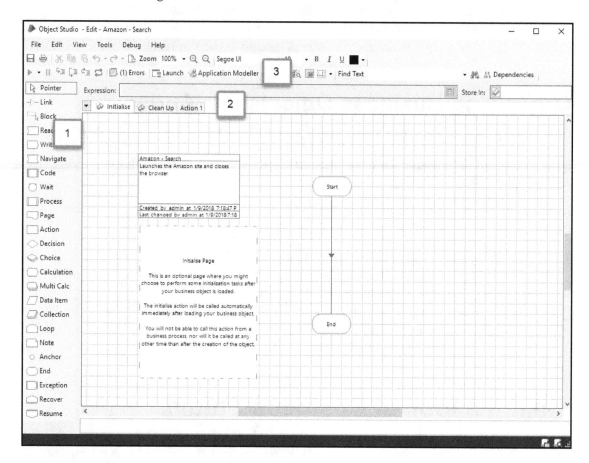

Additional stages available in the Business Studio toolbox

There are new stages to explore in Business Studio. These are as follows:

Stage type	Description
Read	Trains the robot to read the screen. It can look for labels, status reports, and other sorts of messages.
Write	Gets the robot to key text into input boxes.

Navigate	Helps the robot to open and close applications as well as move from screen to screen.
Code	Instructs the robot to execute custom code written in either VB.NET or C#.
Wait	Stops processing for a set amount of time or simply to wait until a certain element appears on the screen.

As we work through the exercises in this and the upcoming chapters, we will become familiar with all these new stages.

Ready, start, action!

Instead of working with pages, as we did in processes, it's all about actions with Business Objects. By default, every Business Object is created with the following actions:

- **Initialize**: This is like the start up script or the do-this-first set of instructions for Business Objects. The most common usage of Initialise is to add global references to code libraries or to insert global methods that are shared across all actions.
- **Clean up**: As the name suggests, this is where you would insert any instructions when the Business Object unloads.
- **Action 1**: An empty action for us to fill in.

We don't usually amend the **Initialise** and **Clean up** actions. The starting point for building a Business Object typically begins with **Action 1**.

Renaming actions

Action 1 is probably not the best name for an action. We wouldn't have any clue about what it does just by looking at the name. Let's rename **Action 1** to something more useful, like **Launch**, for example:

1. With the **Amazon – Search** action opened in Object Studio, right-click on the **Action 1** tab. Choose **Rename**.
2. Give a new name to the action. In our case, enter **Launch**.
3. Click **OK** to close the dialog. **Action 1** has been renamed to **Launch**.

Introducing the Application Modeller

A Business Object acts as the robot's hands and eyes. Through what is called the Application Modeller, we will tell the robot which application it needs to know as we teach it to identify all the parts of the screen that it needs to work with.

We have an action named **Launch,** but it doesn't do anything yet. What we want it to do is to get the robot to open up the Amazon site. Before we do so, we need to tell the robot the following in relation to the Amazon site:

- It is opened using Internet Explorer
- The address of the site is `http://www.amazon.com`

We will give these instructions using the **Application Modeller**:

1. From the toolbar, click **Application Modeller** Application Modeller . The **Application Modeller Wizard** launches.
2. Choose **Define a new application model**. Blue Prism also asks for the name of the application. Keep the suggested name of **Amazon – Search** and click **Next**.
3. We get to choose the type of application with which we are integrating. Since it is Internet Explorer we are interested in, choose **Browser-based Application (Internet Explorer)**. Click **Next**.
4. The next question asks whether we are going to get the robot to launch a fresh instance of Internet Explorer or assume that it is already running. As this is the first time we are launching the browser, choose **A browser that is launched from an executable file**. Click **Next**.

> If you are working with a browser that is already opened, choose the other option – **A browser which is already running**.

5. Tell the robot where to find the Internet Explorer program. It has a suggested path that is the typical location of the `iexplore.exe` file. Unless you have a different setup, accept that default path and click **Next**.
6. The next screen asks for the website address we want to open. Enter `http://www.amazon.com`. Click **Next**.
7. Click **Next** through the rest of the wizard and accept the suggested values until you reach the final screen. Click **Finish**.

8. Back in **Application Modeller**, an empty element named **Element 1** has been created for us. Ignore **Element 1** for now and click **Amazon - Basic** to select it. Notice that all the choices that we have made in the wizard are reflected on the page. You can adjust the values by updating them here, or choose to run the wizard again by clicking on the **Application Wizard** button:

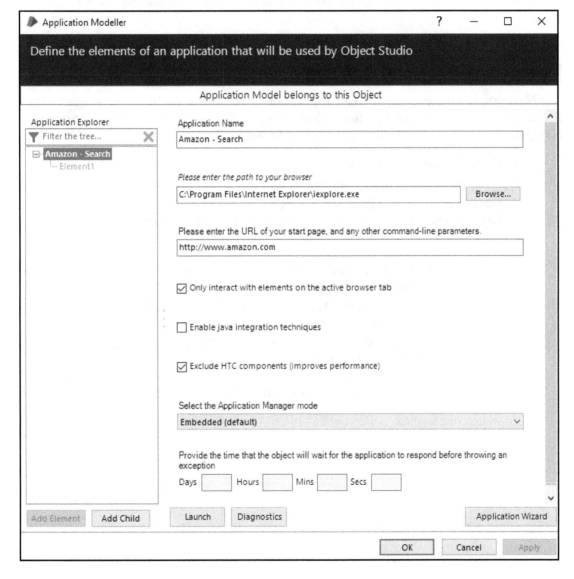

9. Click **OK** to close the **Application Modeller**.

Using the Navigate stage

Application Modeller now contains the details of what our application is about and the page we want to open. However, on its own, it does not do anything with the application. We have got to use it together with the stage blocks on the action page in order for it to be useful. Since we want to open the web page, we will start off by exploring the **Navigate** stage.

Launching applications

The **Navigate** stage is used to open an application or to close it. As the name suggests, it is also used to move from one page to another, as we shall see in later examples. Let's use the **Navigate** stage to launch the Amazon site in Internet Explorer:

1. Open the **Launch** action to edit it.
2. From the toolbox, drag a **Navigate** stage and drop it beneath the **Start** stage.
3. Double-click the **Navigate** stage to open up its properties. Rename the stage **Launch Amazon**. The **Navigate Properties** dialog (shown in the following screenshot) contains the following key sections:

   1. On the left, we see the **Application Explorer**. Every element that we have spied on the page (for now, there's only Element 1) is listed here,
   2. To the right is the **Actions** tab. This is where we will insert the instructions to open the site. The **Element** field is where we specify which part of the website we want to work with. Drag and drop **Amazon - Basic** to the **Element** field.
      The **Action** dropdown lists all the possible things that we can do with the element. As we want to open the site, choose **Launch**.

4. When you are ready, click **OK** to close the dialog, as demonstrated in the following screenshot:

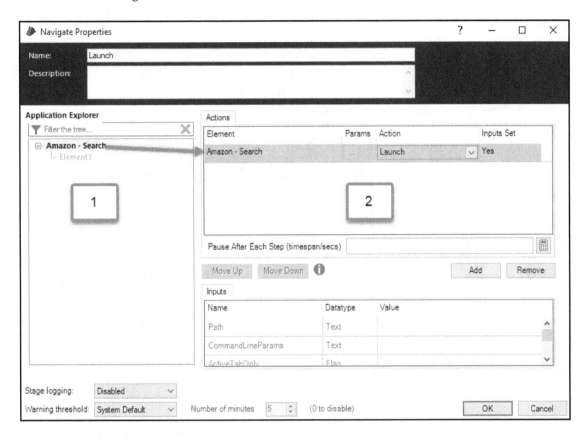

5. Back on the **Launch** action, use the **Link** tool to link all the stages together.

> Press the **Save** button from the toolbar at any time to save your work. Alternatively, press *Alt + S*.

Testing the launch action

Now that we have completed the coding for the **Launch** action, let's give it a test run to see whether it works:

1. Press the **Play** button from the toolbar.
2. Watch the stages move from Start to Launch Amazon. At this point, Internet Explorer opens up with the Amazon website loaded.
3. Finally, the run stops at the **End** stage.

> If you press **Play** immediately after running the object, you will get the error message `Internal: There is no current stage`. To run it again, simply press **Reset,** followed by **Detach,** before pressing **Play**.

Terminating applications

We have an action to launch Internet Explorer. Now, we will create another action to terminate it:

1. To create a new action, right-click anywhere on the action bar. Choose **New**.
2. Name the page **Terminate**. Click **OK**.
3. Drag a **Navigate** stage from the toolbox and drop it between the **Start** and **End** stages.
4. Double-click on the **Navigate** stage to open its properties. Name the stage **Terminate**.
5. As we did in the previous example, drag **Amazon - Search** from Application Explorer and drop it into the **Element** field.
6. This time, in the **Actions** dropdown, choose **Terminate**.
7. Click **OK** to close the dialog. Back at the **Terminate** action page, link all the stages together.

> Running the **Terminate** action is actually the same as killing the process from Task Manager. It's quite a brutal way to close an application. Usually, we will use a more graceful approach, such as pressing *Alt + F + X* to close the Browser. Nevertheless, **Terminate** is an important action often used to quickly close applications when they are no longer required.

Testing the terminate action

Each time you complete an action, you may test it from Business Studio using the following steps:

1. If the application is not opened, click **Launch** from the toolbar to launch it. Once the application launches, the button is replaced by the **Detach** button.
2. Right-click on the stage you want to start from. In this case, we want to test **Terminate**, so we will begin from the **Start** stage of the **Terminate** action. Choose **Set Next Stage**. The stage is highlighted in orange.
3. Press **Play**. Watch the **Terminate** action close Internet Explorer.

Publishing an action

We have finally completed the build of our custom Business Object. However, before it can be used by processes, we need to publish it:

- Right-click on the action's name and choose **Publish** from the context menu.
- Notice that an icon ☁ appears next to the action's name to indicate that it has been published.

Use the preceding steps to publish both the **Launch** and **Terminate** actions.

Using a custom Business Object from a process

We are now ready to integrate the **Amazon - Basic** Business Object that we have just built with the purchasing process from the previous chapters.

Earlier, we saw how to use the internal Business Objects that shipped with Blue Prism in a process. Using a custom-built Business Object, like the **Amazon - Basic** object that we have just completed, is similar. Let's see how it is done:

1. Open the **Weekly purchase of groceries** process that we built earlier.
2. Open the **Search and Add Item to Cart** sub-page. Break the link between the **Loop Input - List of Items to Purchase** stage and the **Note** stage that we added in as a stub earlier.

3. Add an **Action** stage and drop it directly beneath the **Loop Input - List of Items to Purchase** stage. Configure it as follows:
   - **Name:** Launch Amazon
   - **Business Object:** Amazon - Search
   - **Action:** Launch

4. Add another **Action** stage and drop it beneath the note stage that we were using as a stub. Configure it as follows:
   - **Name:** Close Amazon
   - **Business Object:** Amazon - Search
   - **Action:** Terminate

The completed diagram should look as follows:

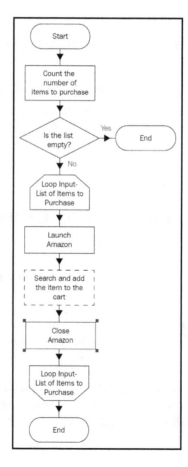

Save the process and give it a test run. Do you see the Amazon site being launched in Internet Explorer for a short while before closing again? We have not actually performed a search of the items added to the cart. We will get right to that in the next chapter.

If you are not able to select the **Launch** and **Terminate** actions from the list of available actions for the **Amazon - Search** object, you might want to try the following:

1. Close the process and open it again. The list of actions available is only loaded when the process is opened for editing. Therefore, if the actions were added or published after the process was opened, the updates will not be reflected in the dropdown.
2. Check that you have published the actions.

What happens if you have multiple applications and you need to swivel from one window to the next in order to perform tasks? To do so, you will have to trigger a **Launch** for each of the applications and not terminate any of them until you are done with them. The controlling process is able to launch several applications at the same time. It can interact with each screen and only trigger a **Terminate** action when it has completed the task.

Summary

We have completed building our first custom Business Object. We saw how to organize newly created Business Objects into folders and rename them. We also launched the Application Modeller wizard to define the application that we are working with. Using the information that we gave about the application, we then used the **Navigate** stage to launch and close it. Finally, we integrated the Business Object into the process and saw how the process uses the **Action** stage to interact with it.

Next up, we will look at spying and how to teach the robot to identify elements such as buttons and text boxes on the screen.

6
Spying Elements

In the previous chapter, we got Amazon up and running by opening the site in Internet Explorer. However, we want to do a lot more than opening websites. In this chapter, we will do the following:

- Teach the robot to spy elements using Application Modeller
- Learn how to tweak the match criteria so that the robot is able to find the elements again
- Add more elements to the Modeller and categorize them
- Learn about the various spy modes available in Blue Prism, including HTML, UI Automation, and region modes

What is spying? Spying is the way to teach the robot to look for elements such as buttons, links, and textboxes on the screen. It acts as the robot's eyes, telling it where to find the items that it needs to click, press, or key text into.

Spying is crucial to the building of business objects. Without spying, the robot will not be able to *see* and interact with the application being modeled.

Spying elements on a web page

One of the tasks performed by the purchasing process is to search the Amazon site for the items to purchase. Before the robot can perform a search, it needs to interact with the following elements, as shown in the following screenshot:

- The search textbox for entering the keywords
- The search button

Let's train the robot to identify these elements on the page by using Application Modeller to spy on it:

1. Open the **Amazon - Search** business object for editing. From the toolbar, click **Application Modeller**.
2. Let's familiarize ourselves with the **Application Modeller** dialog. On the left is the **Application Explorer**. It's a directory that lists all the items that you have spied. At this point, we have not spied any elements. The first element, **Element1**, was automatically created when we ran the wizard.
3. Click on the empty **Element1**. On the left are the **Element Details**. As we have not spied anything yet, what is shown is just a shell.
4. The name, **Element1,** does not tell us much about what it is. In the **Name** field, rename **Element1** to **Textbox - Search**. Adding the element's type to the name (for example, Link, or Button) gives us a good indicator of what it does just by looking at it.
5. Launch the Amazon site by clicking on the **Launch** button from Application Modeller. Try to arrange the Application Modeller and Internet Explorer windows to be side by side in such a way that you can easily see both windows clearly (refer to the following screenshot). Also, notice that the label on the Launch button changes to **Identify**:

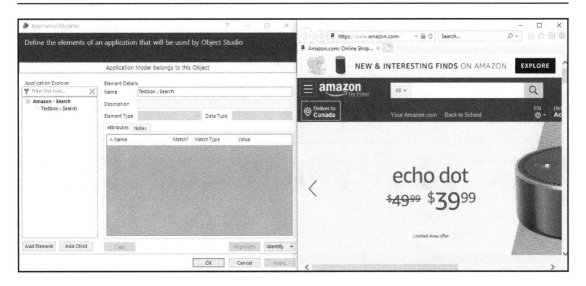

6. We are ready to start spying! Click **Identify**. The identification tool appears as a green box with the words **Using the Identification Tool – (IE HTML mode)**. Now, place your mouse over the Amazon home page. Notice that as you move the mouse, the parts of the screen where the mouse hovers over is highlighted by a green box. We are interested in the search textbox. Place the mouse over the search textbox and wait for the entire box to be highlighted in green. As soon as it appears, press the *Ctrl* key together with a left mouse click.

When spying web pages, always make sure that the **Zoom** setting on Internet Explorer is set to 100%. Otherwise, the highlighting will not work as expected.

7. Back in **Application Modeller**, the **Element Details** panel is automatically filled up, as shown in the following screenshot. Blue Prism makes some assumptions regarding the search textbox:

1. First, take a look at the **Element Type**. The **Element Type** will later determine the actions that you can perform on an element. In this case, Blue Prism says that it is an **HTML Edit**, which is technically correct as we spied a textbox.

2. Next, it says that the **Data Type** is **Text**, which again is correct as we are expecting text to be entered into the search box.

3. Finally, it also makes some guesses about how to correctly identify the Search textbox in the **Attributes** tab. Sort the attributes list by the **Match** column and make a note of the rows that are checked. In a moment, we will learn how to tweak these suggestions. For now, let's just accept what Blue Prism has configured, as shown in the following screenshot:

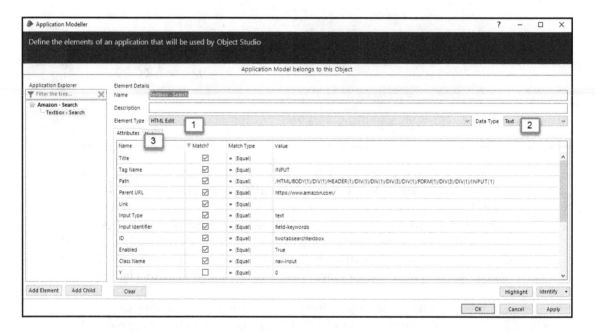

8. The **Highlight** button is very useful for checking to see whether the element can be spied successfully. Over time, if the attributes of the search box change, we can use **Highlight** to see whether we are still able to identify it. Click **Highlight** and observe that the search textbox is highlighted in red. This means that Blue Prism is able to find it based on the match attributes captured earlier:

How does spying work?

A robot does not have real eyes to see what is on the screen. How then is it able to look for elements that it needs to interact with? Here's how it does it for HTML pages:

1. It scans through the page by looking at the HTML source code. A web page is made up of many HTML components. Here is an example of a page that contains a textbox and a button:

```
<HTML>
 <BODY>
 Search: <input type= "text" id= "twotabsearchtextbox" />
 <input type="submit" value="Go" />
 </BODY>
 </HTML>
```

2. The robot breaks the HTML down into elements, such as textboxes, labels, buttons, and links. Each element is defined by a markup tag. For example, a textbox is an `<INPUT/>` tag, while a hyperlink is an `<A/>`.
   Let's take the preceding code, for example. The robot sees a textbox (type=text) with an identifier value of twotabsearchtextbox:
   `<input type= "text" id= "twotabsearchtextbox" />`.
   It also sees a button (`type=submit`) with a value of Go:
   `<input type="submit" value="Go" />`.

3. Using the **Match** attributes, it scans through the entire page to find the element that it wants. Say, for example, that you are looking for the search textbox, then the match attributes to identify it are as follows:
   - **Tag name:** Input
   - **Input type:** Text
   - **ID:** twotabsearchtextbox

4. And if you are looking for the button, you may use the following attributes instead:
   - **Tag name:** Input
   - **Input type:** Submit
   - **Value:** Go

If all this sounds alien to you, not to worry. The good news is that it does not matter if you don't know HTML. The robot interprets the code for you. Earlier, when we spied the Search textbox, we did not have to look at the underlying HTML code for the Amazon site. However, some level of understanding may be required to tweak the match criteria for the robot in order to be able to successfully identify the element and to make the robot resilient to minor updates on the website.

Tweaking the match criteria

Earlier, when we spied the Search textbox, Blue Prism came up with a list of suggested match criteria to correctly identify the element, as shown in the following screenshot:

Attributes	Notes		
Name	▼ Match?	Match Type	Value
Title	☑	= (Equal)	
Tag Name	☑	= (Equal)	INPUT
Path	☑	= (Equal)	/HTML/BODY(1)/DIV(1)/HEADER(1)/DIV(1)/DIV(1)/DIV(3)/DIV(1)/FORM(1)/DIV(2)...
Parent URL	☑	= (Equal)	https://www.amazon.com/
Link	☑	= (Equal)	
Input Type	☑	= (Equal)	submit
Input Identifier	☑	= (Equal)	
ID	☑	= (Equal)	
Enabled	☑	= (Equal)	True
Class Name	☑	= (Equal)	nav-input
Y	☐	= (Equal)	0

All these conditions must be satisfied in order for the robot to locate the Search textbox. What happens if Amazon decides to change the appearance of the textbox and give it a different class name?

Well, we can't hack into Amazon's site and effect the change. For the purposes of the demonstration, let's simulate that by changing the **Class Name** attribute from `nav-input` to `nav-input2`.

Now, click the **Highlight** button again. Oops, are you getting the same error message as the one here?

What just happened? We only changed the value of one of the many match attributes. Why isn't Blue Prism able to find the Search textbox now? The answer lies in the way matching works. Every single item checked in the match criteria must be fulfilled in order for the robot to be able to find it again. If even a single one fails the match test, the element will be deemed to be missing.

It is for this reason that deciding what to check in the match criteria selection is very important. Usually, we will use the following attributes:

1. **Those that uniquely identify the element on a page**: For HTML web pages, most site developers will assign a unique label to each element for better programming. That label is usually called ID and/or name. Developers typically use both attributes when programming a site. To learn more about the **ID** attribute, take a look at this link (`https://www.w3schools.com/tags/att_global_id.asp`).

2. **Those that are unlikely to change over the life span of the page**: Choosing attributes such as `path` may be risky as it gets changed when developers move elements around the page. For example, if the search box gets shifted further up or down the page, its `path` changes. The same can be said, for example, for attributes that describe the look and feel of the element or the value that it contains (for example, **class name** and **value**).

There are no hard and fast rules when selecting the match criteria. It is more an art than a science. It takes a bit of trial and error to get it right. And even if we "think" that we have the correct mix in the bag, the website may change again, causing us to rethink our selection.

Tightening the match criteria

Let's tighten up the match criteria for the Search textbox to make it more robust to changes on Amazon's site. Since the developers at Amazon have used the **ID** and **Input Identifier** attributes to uniquely label the element, we shall get Blue Prism to use these two attributes to look for the search box. Let's tighten the match criteria further:

1. Back in **Application Modeller**, select **Textbox – Search**. Sort the **Attributes** according to the **Match** column such that the matching attributes are listed at the top.
2. Uncheck all the match criteria, except for the following:
    - Input Identifier
    - ID
3. Click **Highlight**. Check that the Search textbox can still be found on the screen.
4. Click **Apply** to save the changes without closing the window.

Now, we have made the robot a lot more resilient to changes to the target website. Unless Amazon changes the **Input Identifier** or **ID** attributes of the element, we should always be able to identify the Search textbox.

 In earlier versions of Blue Prism, the path attribute was commonly used to identify HTML elements, even if they had unique identifiers assigned to it. The main reason for doing so was to improve the speed at which the robot could find the elements. This resulted in the robot being vulnerable to updates on the target website, where the positions of elements may change due to updates. For example, inserting an advertisement on the web page may shift all the elements down one path level, thereby breaking processes. In the recent releases of Blue Prism, the algorithm for identification has been improved greatly such that it is now feasible to identify elements based on identifiers instead of **Path**.

Adding elements

We have successfully spied the search textbox. In order to execute the search, we will need to press the search button as well. Let's proceed to spy the Search button by adding an element to Application Modeller:

1. With the **Textbox - Search** element selected, click **Add Element**. A new empty element named **Element1** is added to Application Explorer. Rename **Element1** to **Button - Search**.
2. Click **Identify** and highlight the **Search** button ⬚. Press *Ctrl* + left mouse click when the button is highlighted in green.
3. Once the button has been identified, tighten the match criteria by unchecking all the matches and leaving only the following:
    *   Tag name
    *   Path
    *   Input type

Hey, wait a minute. Didn't we just mention that the position of the Search button may change, so therefore we don't use the path attribute in the match criteria? It really isn't a hard and fast rule. If you looked at the Search button, it does not have any unique labels, such as **ID** or **Input Identifier**. In this case, in order to quickly identify the search button, path is the surest way to find it.

Categorizing elements

As we build up the Application Modeller and add more elements to the list, it is going to grow and grow. It is not uncommon to have lists that number in the hundreds of elements. Looking for the element that you want to work with becomes a huge exercise akin to looking for a needle in a haystack. One nice bit about elements is that they can be ordered and categorized by nesting them. Observe the following steps to see how it's done:

1. In **Application Explorer**, select **Amazon - Search**. Click **Add Child**. This creates a new element directly beneath the root.

 Alternatively, you could have chosen any of the elements that we created earlier and clicked **Add Element**. This creates the new element at the same level as the other elements.

2. Name the new element **Search**.

3. Drag the two elements that we created previously and drop them on top of the newly created **Search** element. The final result is shown here:

Notice that the **Search** element is grayed out. This indicates that it is just an empty shell and not linked to any spied element. For elements that are used as category labels, it is perfectly fine to leave them empty.

More spy modes

When we spied the Search textbox and button, we used HTML mode. We saw it indicated in a green box when we tried to highlight the elements on the Amazon home page. HTML mode has worked well so far. We were able to identify the elements we needed.

What if the application that we are working with is not a web page but, say, a Windows application such as Microsoft Office? Or perhaps the web page uses modern web technologies that are too dynamic for Blue Prism to find elements using HTML mode.

To solve these common spying issues, Blue Prism supports the following alternative spy modes:

- **Win32 mode** uses the base Windows 32 API to look for elements in an application. It is typically used to spy Windows-based applications.

- **Accessibility mode** uses the Microsoft Active Accessibility (AA) framework. Its origins started when there was a demand for providing alternative means to access a website for automated testing tools. As the tests are automated, we can't rely on someone to control the program using a keyboard and mouse. Therefore, Microsoft built the AA framework for developers to write test scripts that can be executed programmatically. In recent times, AA has been superseded by the **UI Automation framework** (UIA). While Blue Prism still supports AA for backward compatibility, the preference is to use UIA.

- **UI Automation mode** uses **Microsoft's UI Automation** (**UIA**) framework for identifying elements. It is a new framework that offers many improvements over AA.
- **Region mode** is a special way of identifying elements on screen by their actual pixel locations on the screen; for example, the search button is 100 pixels to the left and 50 pixels from the top of the screen.

You can see each mode in action by pressing the *Alt* key while performing the spying operation. The colored box cycles through each mode, changing colors as it does. For example, the Win32 mode box is pink, as shown in the following screenshot:

> ⓘ Using the Identification Tool - (Win32 mode)
>
> Use Ctrl and left-click to select the highlighted item, or Ctrl and right-click to cancel.
>
> Press the Alt key to switch spy modes

There is no rule book to say that we must use one mode of spying over another. Which mode you choose depends on the situation and the nature of the application. Not every website can be spied using HTML mode. A lot of what is *right* is derived through lots of experimentation and trial and error. Typically for websites, you would choose the HTML model. However, as we will see later, we may choose the other spy modes when we are not able to successfully spy the element we need to work with in HTML mode.

UI Automation mode

Let's try out the other spy modes. Observe the following steps to spy the first item that appears in the search results listing using the UI Automation mode:

1. In the search box, enter the keywords to look for any item that you may want to purchase. Later on, we will get the robot to enter the keywords for us. For now, as we are still spying the elements, we will enter it manually. When you are ready, click the Search button and wait for the results to be displayed.
2. Let's create a new element for storing all the elements related to the search results page. Back in Application Explorer, add an element beneath **Amazon – Search**. Name the element **Search Results**. This will be our container for storing all the elements related to the Search Results page.

3. Add another element. This time, place it beneath the **Search Results** element. Name the element **List – First Result**.

4. With **List - First Result** selected, click **Identify**. Back on the Amazon search results page, press ALT until the spy mode switches to **UI Automation mode**. Use it to highlight the first result in the search listing. Press *Ctrl* + left mouse-click when the link is highlighted, as shown in the following screenshot:

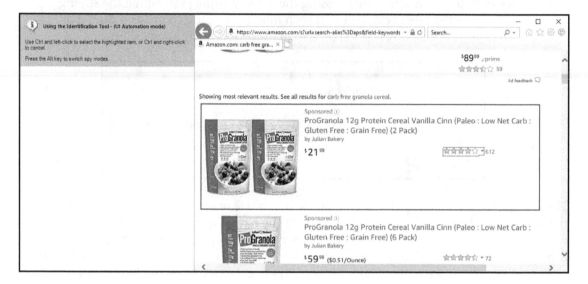

5. Take a look at what was captured by Blue Prism. The **Element Type** is **List Item (UIA),** which indicates that we identified the item using UIA. The match criteria are also different from the ones that were captured when we identified elements using HTML mode. Instead of using HTML property values for matching, Blue Prism is using UIA property values, such as **UIA Control Type** and **UIA Automation Id**.

6. Tweak the match criteria by unchecking all the items except for the following:
   - **UIA Control Type**
   - **UIA Automation Id**

7. In addition, check the following item:
   - **Parent UIA Automation Id**

The completed list of match attributes is as follows:

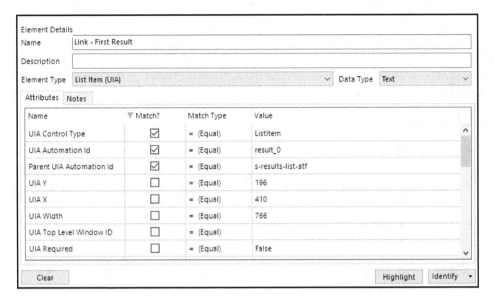

8. Click **Highlight** to check to see whether you are still able to identify the element on the screen. We have successfully spied the first item in the search results!

When spying by identifying does not work

Well, we may not always want to purchase the first item, will we? Besides, if you take a closer look at the item, it is marked as **sponsored**. Do we really want to purchase that? What about the other items in the list? Let's attempt the following steps to spy the entire search results list so that we can program the robot to pick the item that we really want from it:

1. In Application Explorer, select **Search Results** and click **Add Child**. Name the new element **List - Search Results**.
2. Click **Identify** and use the *Alt* key to toggle to **UI Automation mode**.
3. Back on the Amazon search results page, try to highlight the entire search results listing. It's hard to do so. Each time you place your mouse over the list, the best you can capture is a single row of results. However, we need the entire table, so how can we get it?

Let's abandon this approach. Press *Ctrl* + right mouse click to cancel the spy operation.

UI Automation navigator

In cases where it's difficult to locate the element on the screen using the mouse, we have the option of using the navigators. Navigators scan an entire page for elements that can be identified and present it as a list. All we need to do is to select the element that we want from the list. These elements are located in the sub-menu (refer to the following screenshot) that appears when you click on the arrow next to the **Identify** button.

The menu has three options:

- **Spy Element**: This is the default option and is the one that we have used to identify elements in HTML and UIA mode by clicking on them in spy mode.
- **Open Application Navigator**: This option uses the older AA framework to scan the entire page for all the elements that can be identified.
- **Open UI Automation Navigator**: This option also scans the page for elements, but it uses the newer and better UIA framework.

Observe the following steps to use the **UI Automation Navigator** to spy the entire search results list, an element that we were not able to identify using the point and click method:

1. From **Application Explorer**, select the **List - Search Results** element. Click **Identify | UI Automation Navigator**.
2. Wait while the **UI Application navigator** window loads. It might take a while, so just be patient. When the navigator completes loading, scroll through the list of available elements. The list is extensive. Every link, button, label, and picture is captured here.
3. Scan through the list of available elements. What we are looking for is an element that shows the entire search results table. The list is pretty long! In the **Available Elements** section, there is a filter bar. Enter (list) to get all the lists that can be seen by the robot on the page. It may take some time for the results to show up.

In the version of Blue Prism at the time of writing, this particular function wasn't working too well. Using the filter caused Blue Prism to be unresponsive. If this is what you observe as well, then skip this step and move on to *Step 4*. Instead of inspecting the filtered list, you will have to look at the complete listing.

4. Look through the filtered results in the **Available Elements** section and click on any element named **(list)**. As you click on the element, notice that the **Attribute** panel gets updated with that element's values. Also, the element that you have selected is highlighted in red in the website.

For each element that you select, look at the **Attributes** section. Keep a watch out for the **AutomationId** value. When you find the **(list)** element with an **AutomationId** value of `s-results-list-atf` (see the following), we have found our element:

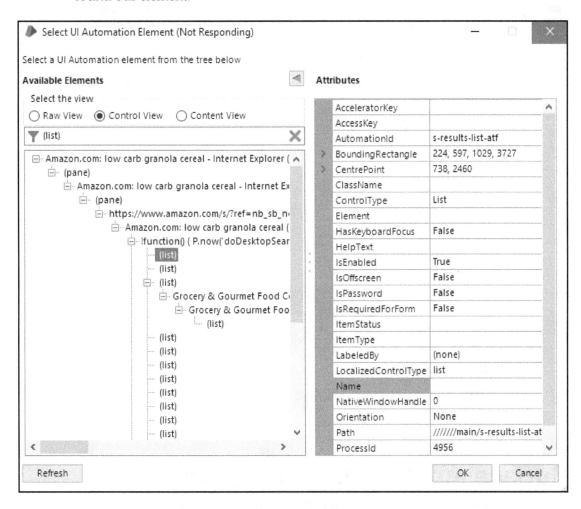

If you are scanning through the complete listing of elements, the search results are located one third of the way down the list somewhere along the path **Amazon.com** | **(pane)** | **Amazon.com** | **(pane)** | **https://www.amazon.com** | **Amazon.com (pane)** | **!funcion()** | **(list)**.

5. Once you locate the element that defines the list of search results, click **OK** to close the navigator.

6. Back in **Application Modeller**, uncheck all the match attributes and leave only **UIA Automation Id** checked.

Also, note that Blue Prism has identified the element type to be **List** instead of just a **List Item,** like the element that gets only the first result. This is an important distinction later on when we try to read the table as it will give us the option to store all the items in a collection that we can loop through to decide which one we want to purchase. The following screenshot shows the completed dialog:

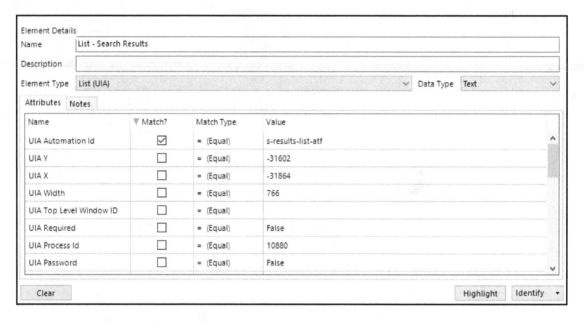

Just to be doubly sure, click **Highlight**. Notice that the entire search results table is highlighted. We got the full result set!

Surface automation with region mode

Methods of identification through point and click and using the navigator works most of the time to find the elements that we need to interact with. They work especially well if the application is installed on the same computer as the robot. However, we are seeing more and more technologies that work off a remote machine. The application is installed on a server somewhere in the network and what is sent to your computer is just an image that you can interact with. Examples of such applications (also known as **thin-clients**) include Citrix, Microsoft Terminal Services, and Mainframes.

In such special cases, we need to fall back on the good old method of looking at the position of the element on the screen to figure out where they are. This method of spying is also known as surface automation. The spy mode that supports surface automation is region mode.

Observe the following steps to try out region mode. Note that we are using the Amazon site simply as an example. It does not require surface automation to identify elements; however, this also shows that surface automation can be deployed for regular applications as well. Here, we will use region mode to spy the top menu of the Amazon site:

1. Back in **Application Modeller**, create a new element beneath **Amazon - Search**. Give it the name **Top Menu**.
2. With **Top Menu** selected, create Identify. Press **ALT** until the spy mode switches to the light brown colored **region mode**. Hover over the Amazon site until a brown box is drawn around the entire page. Press *Ctrl* + left mouse click to select it.
3. Immediately after the area is captured, the Blue Prism Region Editor dialog opens with the screenshot of what we captured in it. From the toolbar, click **Region**. Use it to draw a hashed box over the Amazon logo, as shown in the following screenshot. When you release the mouse, notice that the properties pane on the right-hand side gets updated with the coordinates of the area that we have drawn.
4. Click **OK** to close the **Region Editor**:

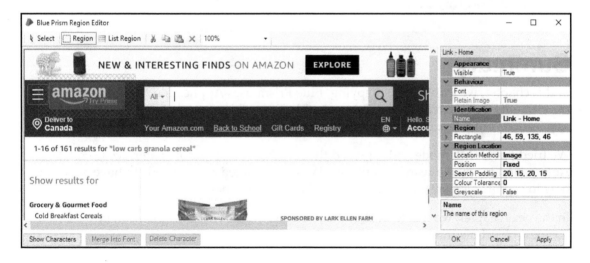

5. Give the element a more meaningful name. Rename it from **Region 1** to **Link - Home**. Take a look at the match criteria for **Link - Home**. The matching criteria are specific to the image that we captured earlier. Some key properties to note are the following:

- **Location method**: The default option in Blue Prism 6.0 onward is **Image**. We took a screen capture of the area and used a rectangle to identify which part of the image contains the element.
- **Image search padding**: Did you see the hashes when we drew the rectangle around the home button? That is the additional space within which Blue Prism will look for the image. Should it move within this margin, a match is still found. You can adjust the values here and make the numbers bigger so that it extends across the entire screen.

6. Ensure that the Amazon website is fully visible on the screen. Surface automation requires that the screen be seen. If the window is hidden, it won't work. Click **Highlight** and observe that the home page logo is correctly identified.

7. We are done with spying for now. Click **OK** to close **Application Modeller**. Save the **Amazon - Search** business object.

The study of surface automation is rather extensive. Here, we have only explored one way to use it. There are advanced techniques to capture by coordinates, perform OCR, and so on. To find out more about surface automation, take a look at the following link (`https://portal.blueprism.com/system/files/2018-04/Surface%20Automation%20-%20Basic%20Training.pdf`).

Summary

In this chapter, we learned about spying. Blue Prism uses Application Modeller to define the elements that the robot has to interact with. To be able to work with the various types of applications out there, Blue Prism offers several spy modes.

We tried out HTML mode and captured the search box and button. Later, we used UI Automation to spy the search results list. We also sampled region mode to have an idea of how to capture elements that can't be found using other means.

In the next chapter, we will look at how the elements that we have spied can be used in the business object diagram.

Write, Wait, and Read 7

In the previous chapter, we spied all the elements that we want to work with. Now, let's get the robot to interact with them. Using Business Studio, we will build a new search action that will enter keywords into the **Search text** box and click on the **Search** button to trigger the search, after which, it will get the list of search results and pick out the item to purchase and add it to the cart.

To put it all together, we will make use of the following new stages in Object Studio:

- Write
- Wait
- Read

Creating the search action

Let's have a quick recap on the business object that we are building.

We want to do the following:

- Search for the product by entering its name in the **Search text** box and clicking on the **Search** button
- Once the search results are displayed, we will get the listing and pick out the item that we want to purchase

To store this logic, let's observe the following steps to add a new action to the **Amazon - Search** business object:

1. Open **Amazon - Search** in Business Studio for editing.
2. Add a new action and give it the name **Search.** Open the **Search** action page for editing, and now we are ready to roll.

Writing to text boxes

Given a list of items to purchase, we need to enter the keywords to find the item that we want to purchase. To do that, observe the following steps in order to use the **Write** stage to enter text in online forms:

1. With the **Search** action page opened, add a new **Data Item** to the diagram. We will use it to temporarily store the search keywords. Give it the following property values:
   - **Name**: Keywords
   - **Data Type**: Text
   - **Initial Value**: Low Carb Granola Cereal

2. Drag and drop the **Write** stage beneath the **Start** stage. Double-click on the **Write** stage to open the **Write Properties** dialog and configure it as follows:
   - In the **Name** field, rename the stage to Enter search keywords.
   - From **Data Explorer**, drag **Keywords** into the **Value** field.
   - From **Application Explorer**, drag **Textbox – Search** into the **Element** field.

   When done, click **Ok** to close the dialog.

3. Back in the diagram, use the **Link** tool to link all the stages together. The completed diagram should appear as follows:

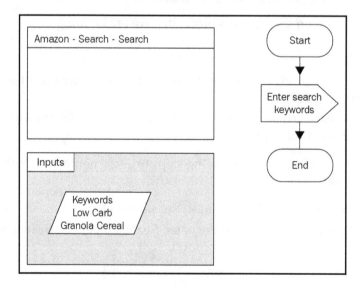

Let's run the action to see whether it works. If you have not already done so, click the **Launch** button on the toolbar to launch the Amazon site in Internet Explorer. Once the site loads, right-click on the **Start** stage and choose **Set Next Stage**. Finally, click **Run** from the toolbar. Did you see the text **Low Fat Granola Cereal** being entered in the **Search text** box?

If there are multiple text boxes on the same form, you can use the same **Write** stage to enter all the text values at the same time. To do so, click on the **Add** button in the **Writer Properties** dialog. You can then specify another value to write and the text box to write it to.

Clicking buttons

The keywords are in the **search** box. All we need to do now is to click on the **Search** button. Earlier, we used the **Navigate** stage to launch/terminate Internet Explorer. Observe the following steps to use the same **Navigate** stage to act as a robotic hand to click on buttons:

1. With the **Search** action page opened for editing, break the link between **Enter search keywords** and **End**.
2. Drag a **Navigate** stage and drop it beneath the **Enter search keywords** stage.
3. Double-click on the **Navigate** stage to open its properties:
    - Give it the name `Click search button`.
    - In the **Actions** panel, drag **Button – Search** from **Application Explorer** and drop it into the **Element** field.
    - In the **Action** dropdown, choose **Click Centre**.

Click **OK** to close the dialog.

4. Finally, use the **Link** tool to link all the stages together, as shown here:

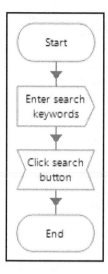

Give it a test run and see that this time, apart from just entering the keywords in the **Search text** box, the robot also clicks on the **Search** button to trigger the search.

The Wait stage

Did you notice that it takes a second or so for the search results page to load fully? As human users, before we type in boxes or click on links, intuitively, we know that we have to wait for the page to complete loading before we can do anything. Robots are not like that at all. If we don't stop it from doing so, the robot will attempt to look for the search results immediately after clicking the **Search** button. All pages take time to load, even if only for a split second. Robots do not wait and even before the page is fully loaded, it would assume that there were no results to be found.

This is where we introduce the **Wait** stage. It is a very handy action to slow the robot down in everything it does at the appropriate time. It is also used to check that the element has been loaded on the page before the robot interacts with it. Let's observe the following steps to teach the robot to wait for the search results to be fully loaded before attempting to read it:

1. In the **Search** action page, break the link between **Click search button** and **End**.
2. Drag and drop a **Wait** stage beneath the **Click Search button** stage. Notice that when you drag and drop a **Wait** stage onto the page, it shows up as a wait-time out pair (refer to the following diagram). The **Time Out** stage is an important part of the design. Without it, the robot may get stuck in an infinite loop, just waiting. In a moment, we will see how we can get the robot to pause for a pre-defined number of seconds, after which, it will time out:

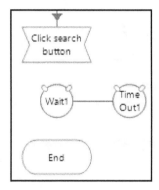

3. Double-click on the **Wait1** circle to open the **Wait Properties** dialog. Rename the element to **Wait for search results**.
4. In the **Actions** panel, notice that a row has already been added for you. Fill it up as follows:
   - From **Application Explorer**, drag the **List – Search Results** element into the **Element** field.
   - In the **Condition** dropdown, select **Check Exists.**
   - Set **Value** to `True`.
5. Finally, at the bottom of the dialog, set the **Timeout** to be `10` seconds. The completed dialog is shown in the following screenshot. Click **OK** when done to close the dialog.
   We've just configured the **Wait** Stage to look for the element, **List - Search Results,** on the screen. As soon as the results listing appears on the page, the robot will stop waiting. We have also set a time limit of 10 seconds. If the page takes more than 10 seconds to load, the stage will time out.

6. Back at the **Search** action page, notice that a little circle has been added between the **Wait** and **Time Out** stages. This indicates that it needs to wait for one element on the screen. The more elements you add to the **Actions** section, the more little circles will show up here.

7. If, for some reason, the search results do not appear, something must have happened that warrants someone to take a closer look. In order to alert a human, we will get the robot to throw an exception back to the controlling process. Drag an **Exception** stage from the toolbox and drop it next to the **Time Out** stage. Double-click on the **Exception** stage and fill in the following property values:

- **Name:** Exception
- **Exception Type:** System Exception
- **Exception Detail:** "Search results took too long to load"

The completed dialog appears as follows. When done, click **OK** to close it:

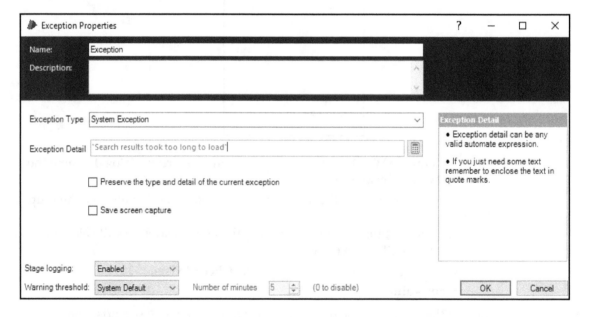

8. Use the **Link** tool to link all the stages together. The completed diagram looks as follows:

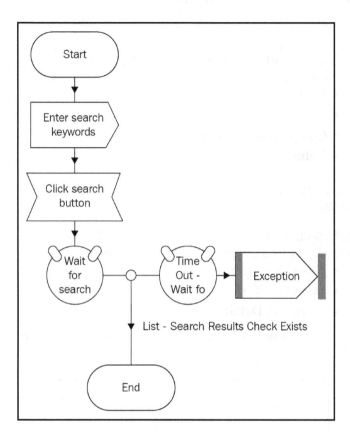

The **Wait** stage has been successfully added to the diagram. Now, when you test the Search action, it will wait for the search results to be fully loaded before hitting the **End** stage.

Always use a Wait stage whenever the screen changes

Take a closer look at the diagram. Do you see any other areas that might benefit from a **Wait** stage? Yes, you got that right: the robot should check to see whether the search box has been loaded before entering the keywords. When the Amazon page first loads, it appears to load very quickly. Instinctively, we know to wait for the search box to be fully loaded before we start to type in it.

However, robots will need to be taught when the page is loaded. To do so, we will observe the following steps and use the Wait stage again:

1. In the **Search** action page, break the link between the **Start** and **Enter search keywords** stages.

2. Add a **Wait** stage after the **Start** stage. Name the **Wait** stage **Wait for search text box**. In the **Actions** panel of the **Wait** stage, configure the following:
   - **Element**: `Textbox – Search`
   - **Condition**: `Check Exists`
   - **Comparison**: `= (Equal)`
   - **Value**: `True`

   Leave the **Timeout** value to be 5 seconds. We don't expect the load time of the Amazon site to be longer than that.

3. Add an **Exception** stage next to the **Time Out - Wait for Search text box** stage. Assign the **Exception** stage the following property values:
   - **Name**: `Exception`
   - **Exception Type**: `System Exception`
   - **Exception Detail**: `"Search text box took too long to load"`

4. Finally, use the **Link** tool to link all the stages together. The completed diagram is shown here:

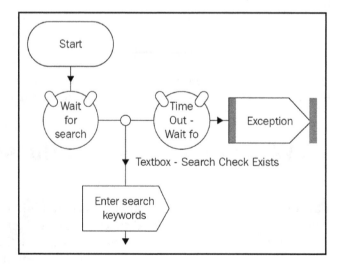

Now, the robot will wait for the text box to be loaded before attempting to enter keywords in it.

 Estimating the wait time can be hard. That's because some sites have variable load times. A page could load in 5 seconds today, but tomorrow, it might take 15 seconds. It's okay to allow for longer wait times to cater for slow days. In the event that the page loads faster than the time out, the process will just exit the **Wait** stage.

The Read stage

We used the **Write** stage to enter text into the search box. Now, let's explore the **Read** stage and see how we can use it to read what is on the screen. In the process that we are building, we have completed loading the search results. We shall now use the following steps to teach the robot to read the listing and pick out the item that we want to purchase using the Read stage:

1. On the **Search** action page, break the link between the **Wait for search results** stage and the **End** stage.
2. Drag a **Read** stage from the toolbar and drop it just above the **End** stage.
3. Double-click on the newly added **Read** stage. In the **Properties** dialog, configure it as follows:
   - **Name:** Read search results
4. In the **Actions** panel, a single row has already been added for you. Perform the following actions:
   - **Element**: Drag the **List – Results** element from **Application Explorer** and drop it into the **Element** field.
   - **Data**: Choose **Get All Items**
   - **Store In field**: Enter **Search Results**. Click on the **Data Item** icon to create the collection.

The completed dialog is shown in the preceding diagram. When you are done, click **OK** to close the dialog.

5. Back at the **Search** action page, link the little circle in the **Wait** stage to the **Read search results** stage. Finally, link the **Read search results** stage to **End** so that the diagram appears as follows:

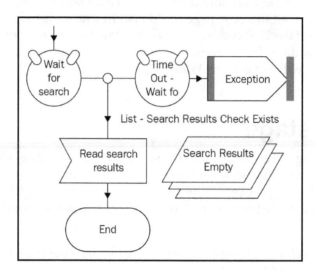

Test out the updated Search action. After the robot runs through the **Read Search results** stage, the **Search Results** collection gets filled with rows of data containing the search results. In our case, there were 20 items found (your results might differ).

Double-click on the **Search Results** collection and look at the **Current Values** tab. We get to see the entire listing, as shown in the following screenshot:

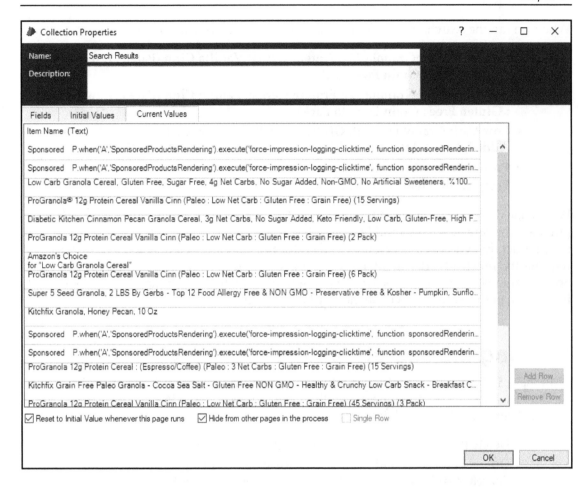

The search yielded 20 results. The number might be different for you but the point is that there are many products to choose from. Which one do we purchase? Do we go with the first result? Or the cheapest? Or the one with the most recommendations? It really is up to you to decide the algorithm that the robot is going to use when selecting the product.

Let's take a closer look at the top five search results. Remember, we searched for **Low Carb Granola Cereal**.

When we ran the search, the top four results in our search were as follows:

- **Sponsored: ProGranola 12g Protein Cereal Vanilla Cinn (Paleo : Low Net Carb : Gluten Free : Grain Free) (2 Pack)**
- **Sponsored: ProGranola 12g Protein Cereal Vanilla Cinn (Paleo : Low Net Carb : Gluten Free : Grain Free) (6 Pack)**
- **Low Carb Granola Cereal, Gluten Free, Sugar Free, 4 g Net Carbs, No Sugar Added, Non-GMO, No Artificial Sweeteners, 100% Natural, No Preservatives**
- **ProGranola® 12g Protein Cereal Vanilla Cinn (Paleo : Low Net Carb : Gluten Free : Grain Free) (15 Servings)**

Which one do we pick? Imagine for a moment that you are really shopping on the site to purchase the cereal. What would be going through your mind as you look at the list to pick the product that you want? Personally, I'd go for the non-sponsored items. If a product requires too much advertisement, it's just not good enough to get sold on its own merits. So, for demonstration purposes, we are going to pick the first result that is not a sponsored item. And, in this case, that will be the third item on the list.

Reading the search results

With the search results neatly tucked into a collection, and with some idea on which product we are going to purchase, we will proceed to observe the following steps in order to train the robot to pick it out on its own:

1. Delete the link between the **Read search results** stage and the **End** stage.
2. Drag a **Loop** stage and place it after **Read search results**. Name the stage **Loop Search Results**. Configure it to iterate the **Search Results** collection.
3. Add a **Data Item** to the diagram. Assign it the following property values:
   - **Name:** RowCount
   - **Data Type:** Number
   - **Initial Value:** 0

We will use **RowCount** to keep track of the row where the item we want to purchase is located. If all goes well in our little example, the item we want to purchase is in the third row. Therefore, when the robot is done, **RowCount** should contain the value 3.

4. Between the **Loop Search Results** stage, add a **Calculation** stage. Assign it the following property values:

- **Name**: Increase RowCount
- **Expression**: [RowCount] + 1
- **Store Result In**: RowCount

Here, we just want to use RowCount to keep track of which row in the **Search Results** collection we are looking at.

5. Next, we will decide whether or not the row contains the product that we want. Remember, we want to get the first product that is not a sponsored item. Drag a **Decision** stage and drop it beneath the **Increase RowCount** stage. Configure its properties as follows:

- **Name**: Is it a sponsored product?
- **Expression**: InStr([Search Results.Item Name], "Sponsored")>0 OR InStr([Search Results.Item Name], "Amazon's Choice")>0

We use the InStr() function to search for the word **Sponsored** or **Amazon's Choice** in the product's name. If any of these words exists, InStr() will give us the location of the text in the form of a number. For example, if the product is described as the following:

Sponsored: ProGranola 12g Protein Cereal Vanilla Cinn (Paleo :
Low Net Carb : Gluten Free : Grain Free) (2 Pack)

Then InStr() will return a value of 1 because the word **Sponsored** appears at the start of the text.

If it can't find the word **Sponsored**, and no match is found, InStr() will return a value of 0. Therefore, if the result of the expression is a number that is greater than 0, we will assume that it is a sponsored product.

6. Add a **Note** stage to the right of the **Is it a sponsored product?** stage. Assign it the text **Click on the item**. We will use it as a stub to simulate the actual clicking of the item once we have decided to purchase it.

7. Finally, link all the stages together, as shown in the following diagram:

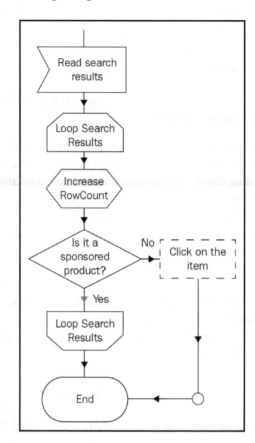

Run and test the action again. We managed to find the first non-sponsored item in the third item of the list. At the end of the run, **RowCount** contained the value 3. It might be a different row for you, depending on what is available on Amazon's website at the time of your search. What we have done is just an example of how a robot can interpret the results that it reads. The string manipulation functions, such as InStr(), are often used to decide the path the robot will take once it has read the text on the screen.

Using dynamic match attributes

We entered the keywords, triggered the search, got some results, sifted through the results, and finally found the item that we want to purchase. How can we get the robot to click on it to get to the product page so that we can add it to the cart?

The problem with the spying methods that we have utilized so far is that it assumes that the item that we want to click on is fixed: if we just want the first item on the list, we just spy it and get the robot to click on it.

In the case of the search results, the position of the item that we want to purchase may vary. Today, it is found in row 3. Tomorrow, it may be in row 5. It is not fixed. The final answer depends on what appears in the listing at the time the search is triggered.

How can we pass the information about which row to click on to the robot? To do this, we need to perform a dynamic match. This part of the process might be a little trickier than the others. Don't worry; we will take you through it step by step, as outlined here:

1. From the toolbar, click **Application Modeller** to open it.
2. Add a new element under **Search Results**. Name it **Link – Item to Purchase**.
3. Click **Identify** and use the *Alt* key to toggle the spy mode to **HTML**. Select the link to the first item in the search results. Select the hyperlink as shown here:

4. Back in **Application Modeller**, uncheck all the match criteria except for **Path**. Take a closer look at the value stored in **Path**. It should look something like the following code:

```
/HTML/BODY(1)/DIV(1)/DIV(2)/DIV(1)/DIV(3)/DIV(2)/DIV(1)/DIV(4)/
DIV(1)/DIV(1)/UL(1)/LI(1)/DIV(1)/DIV(1)/DIV(1)/DIV(2)/DIV(1)/DIV
(1)/A(1)/H2(1)
```

   Don't worry about what this means. We will make use of it later on. For now, copy out the entire code and paste it somewhere convenient, like Notepad.

5. Change the **Match Type** for the **Path** attribute to **Dynamic**. Notice that the **Value** column gets grayed out. This means that **Application Modeller** will no longer read the value that is stored there. It will instead get the value from the action diagram. More on that in a while.
6. We are done with **Application Modeller**. Click **OK** to close it.
7. In the **Search** action page, delete the Note stub **Click on the item** that we were using as a placeholder earlier.

8. Drag a **Calculation** stage and drop it next to the **Is it a sponsored product?** stage. Name the calculation stage **Get the path of the product's page**.

We have defined an element to store the search result, but we still have yet to tell the robot which item to click. Now, let's look at that complex-looking HTML path that we extracted earlier. Remember we got this from spying the link to the first product in the search results listing. Notice the section highlighted in bold. In HTML speak, `LI` refers to a list item. Therefore, `LI(1)` points to the first item in the list:

```
/HTML/BODY(1)/DIV(1)/DIV(2)/DIV(1)/DIV(3)/DIV(2)/DIV(1)/DIV(4)/DIV(1)/DIV(1
)/UL(1)/LI(1)/...
```

This means that in order to get to the third item in the list, we simply replace `LI(1)` with `LI(3)`. Copy the HTML path that we obtained earlier and paste it into the **Expression** box. Remember to add double quotes around it. Look for the `LI(1)` part of the path and replace the number 1 with `" & [RowCount] & "`, so that the final expression is as follows:

```
"/HTML/BODY(1)/DIV(1)/DIV(2)/DIV(1)/DIV(3)/DIV(2)/DIV(1)/DIV(4)/DIV(1)/
DIV(1)/UL(1)/LI(" & [RowCount] &
")/DIV(1)/DIV(1)/DIV(1)/DIV(2)/DIV(1)/DIV(1)/A(1)/H2(1)"
```

In the **Store Result In** field, enter `Product Path` and click on the **Data Item** icon to automatically create it. The completed dialog should appear as follows:

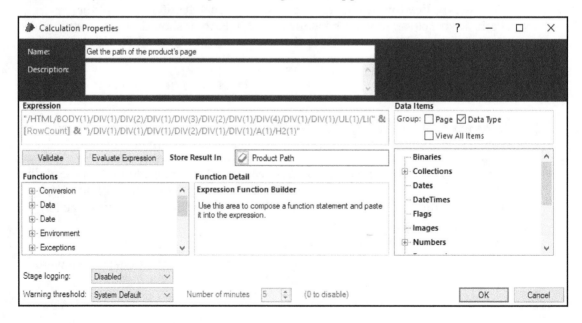

9. Place a **Navigate** stage next to the **Get the path of the product's page** stage:

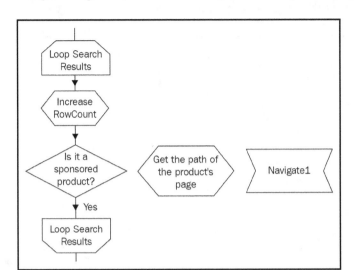

10. Rename the **Navigate1** stage to **Click on the item to purchase**. In its **Actions** panel, drag **Link – Item to Purchase** from **Application Explorer** to the **Element** field. In the **Action** dropdown, choose **Click Center**.

11. Notice that the **Params** button ⬚ is clickable. Click on it and the **Application Element Parameters** dialog opens. Remember that we made the **Path** attribute a dynamic one? It is for this reason that we are now able to define what its value is. Drag **Product Path** from the right-hand panel to the **Value** field.

12. When done, click **OK** twice to close all the opened dialogs. Now, use the **Link** tool so that the diagram appears as follows:

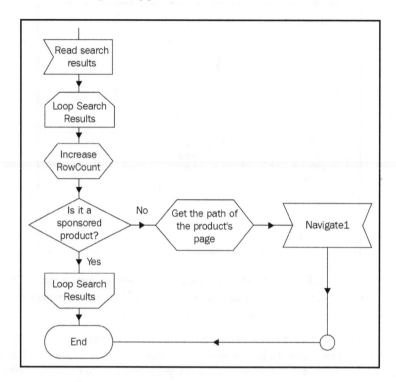

13. Publish the **Search** action so it can be used from within a process. Save the business object.

Now, run the action again. Notice that the robot does not click on the first item it finds (unless that also happens to be the one that you are looking for!). It does what you have taught it to do and clicks on the first non-sponsored item. Did it bring you to the correct product page?

Actions have inputs and outputs too

All throughout the build of our Search action diagram, we have hardcoded the search keywords to be "Low Fat Granola Cereal". That worked well for testing and building up the Business Object. However, we aren't going to restrict our shopping to just that one thing. In our original design, the purchasing process gets the list of shopping from an external list (say, that piece of paper stuck on the fridge). We should feed that list to the Search action, instead of fixing it to "Low Fat Granola Cereal".

To do so, we add inputs to the action, just like we did so earlier for processes, as shown in the following steps:

1. Open the Search action diagram for editing.
2. Double-click on the **Start** stage. In the **Start Properties**, click **Add**. A new row in the **Inputs** list is added.
3. In the **Inputs** field, enter the following values:
    - **Name:** Keywords
    - **Description**: Keywords used to search for the product to purchase on Amazon's site.
    - **Data Type**: Text
4. Drag and drop the **Keywords** data item from the Data Explorer on the right-hand panel to the **Store In** field. The completed dialog appears as follows:

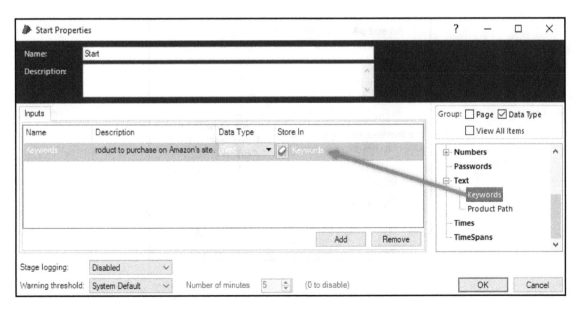

5. Click **OK** when done to close the dialog.

6. Back at the **Search** action diagram, clear the initial value that we entered previously for the **Keywords** data item.

Later on, when we add the Search action to the process diagram, we will be able to specify the keywords that we want to use in its inputs.

Try it yourself – clicking Add to Cart

Alright, we have entered the keywords, triggered the search, and clicked on the item that we want to purchase. All that needs to be done is to click on the **Add to Cart** button. In this section, we will put to use all the knowledge that we have gained in the earlier sections to build up the logic for clicking the **Add to Cart** button.

On the Amazon site, most products have an **Add to Cart** button on the product page. This is the easiest scenario for the robot. It just needs to click **Add to Cart** and it's done. However, some product pages do not have an **Add to Cart** button. Instead, Amazon has a subscription scheme for groceries. They prefer that you make repeated purchases by automatically having the item delivered to your house on a regular basis. While this is a really neat idea, our robot will need to make a decision about what to do when it sees the subscription options. To simplify the problem, we will get the robot to select the **One-time purchase** option wherever it is available (refer to the following screenshot):

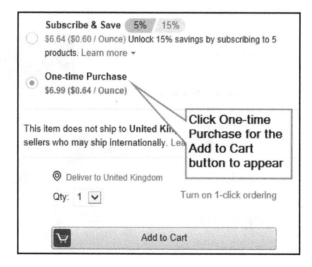

The entire checkout process is actually a lot more complicated when you get down to the details. Some of the items may not ship to your destination country, or may require a minimum quantity to purchase, and so on. These are all considered exceptions, as our robot does not yet know how to handle these situations.

Are you ready to start building the logic to add the item to the cart? As a review, try out the following steps and see whether you are able to build it yourself:

1. First, create a new action page. Give it the name **Add to Cart**.
2. Next, open **Application Modeller** and create a new category element named **Product Page**. Spy and identify the following elements in HTML mode with the corresponding match attributes. The following table provides the details:

No.	Name	Select only these match attributes
1	Button – Add to Cart	• Input Identifier • ID
2	Radio Button – One-time Purchase	• Value • Tag Name
3	Link – Product Title	• Tag Name • ID

Use the following diagram as a reference to identify each of the aforementioned elements:

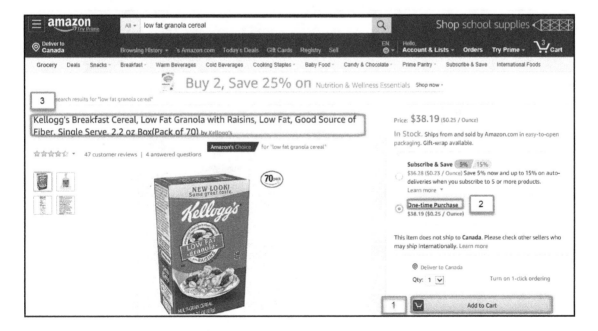

3. Back at the Amazon product page, manually click on the **Add to Cart** button. Notice that we get a message **Added to your cart**. From **Application Modeller**, add another element under the **Product Page** node. Name the new element **Label - Added to your cart**. Spy the message in UI automation mode. This is the element that will let us know whether or not the item has been successfully added to the cart. Retain the following match criteria:

- UIA name
- UIA control type

When you are ready, click **OK** to close **Application Modeller**.

Why did we spy the **Added to cart** message in UI automation mode instead of HTML mode, as we did for the others? That's the thing about spying. Remember there's no right or wrong answer. The reason for choosing UI automation mode is because we want to know whether or not the **Added to your cart** message is visible on the screen. Amazon has the message loaded but kept hidden unless the **Add to Cart** button is clicked. Using HTML mode, we will always pick out all the items that are loaded, but not necessarily visible. The UI automation mode will only find visible items, which is just what we need in this scenario.

4. Back on the canvas, add stages, as shown in the following diagram:

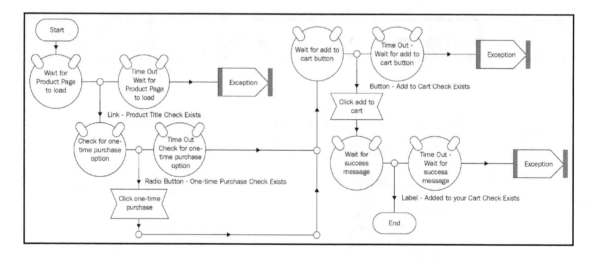

Assign them the property values given in the following table:

Stage name	Type	Property	Value
Wait for Product Page to load	Wait	Timeout	5
		Element	Link – Product Title
		Condition	Check Exists = True
Exception – Wait for Product Page to Load	Exception	Exception Type	System Exception
		Exception Detail	"Product page did not load within the specified time"
Check for one-time purchase option	Wait	Timeout	1
		Element	Radio Button – One-time Purchase
		Condition	Check Exists = True
Click one-time purchase	Navigate	Element	Radio Button – One-time Purchase
		Action	Click Centre
Wait for **add to cart** button	Wait	Timeout	3
		Element	Button – Add to Cart
		Condition	Check Exists = True
Exception – Wait for **add to cart** button	Exception	Exception Type	System Exception
		Exception Detail	"Add to cart button did not load within the specified time"
Click **add to cart**	Navigate	Element	Button - **Add to Cart**
		Action	Click Centre
Wait for success message	Wait	Timeout	5
		Element	Label – Added to your Cart
		Condition	Check Exists = True
Exception – Wait for success message	Exception	Exception Type	System Exception
		Exception Detail	"Failed to add item to the cart"

- Let's add a **Success** flag as an output field to indicate whether or not we were able to successfully add the item to the cart. In the **End** stage, add an output field with the following properties:
    - **Name:** Success

- **Description**: `Flag to indicate whether the operation was successful.`
- **Data Type**: `Flag`
- **Get Value From**: `Click on the Data Item icon to automatically create it.`

When we learn to deal with exceptions in the later chapters of the book, we will populate the **Success** flag.

6. Save and publish the **Add to Cart** action.

Putting it all together

We have completed building the Search action. Let's observe the following steps to integrate what we have done back in the purchasing process that we built earlier:

1. Open the **Weekly purchase of groceries** process. Edit the page **Search and Add Item to Cart**.
2. Delete the note stage, **Search and add the item to the cart**, that we used as a stub.
3. Drag an **Action** and drop it between the **Launch Amazon** and **Close Amazon** stages. Configure it as follows:
   - **Name**: `Search`
   - **Business Object**: `Amazon - Search`
   - **Action**: `Search`

We need to specify the name of the product that we want to purchase as an input. Remember that we stored the list of items to purchase in a collection called **Input - List of Items to Purchase**. We also named the column that stores the names **Item Name**. Therefore, in the **Inputs** panel, enter `[Input - List of Items to Purchase.Item Name]` as the value for the **Keywords**. The period (`.`) is used to get the specific column value in a collection.

4. Next, add another **Action** stage beneath the **Search** stage. Assign it the following property values:
   - **Name**: `Add to Cart`
   - **Business Object**: `Amazon - Search`
   - **Action**: `Add to Cart`

In the **Outputs** panel, we have the **Success** flag. Click on the **Data Item** icon to automatically create the **Success** data item that will indicate whether the item has been successfully added to the cart.

5. Link it all together. The completed diagram within the **Loop Input - List of Items to Purchase** appears as follows:

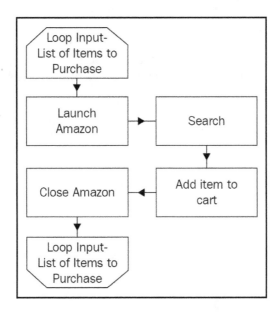

And we are ready to give the process a test run. When you run it, notice that items are now being added to the cart. At the end of the process, check your shopping cart. Did it successfully add everything?

Summary

The skills that you have picked up in this chapter will take you a long way in designing and building your own business objects. We looked at how we can use the **Write** stage to enter text in text boxes. Next, we used the **Read** stage to pick up text on the screen. The robot can be taught to understand the text by clever use of string functions and **Decision** stages. Finally, we learned about the **Wait** stage and how it can be used to check for the existence of elements on the screen before we interact with them.

We concluded the chapter with a self-guided tutorial that serves as a review on all the topics that we have learned so far. We hope you had as much fun as we did building the object.

In the next chapter, we will take a look at how we can read the **Shopping** list from an Excel spreadsheet.

8
Working with Excel

Microsoft Excel is the ubiquitous software that helps us to organize data into spreadsheets that contain rows and columns of data. Almost anyone who owns a Windows-based personal computer has probably used it to keep track of data, perform calculations, or create graphs and charts.

With the extensive use of Excel in our everyday lives, it is not surprising that Blue Prism is shipped with a library that opens up the world of Excel to robots. Using the library, the robots are able to perform some of the common things that we do with Excel:

- Open workbooks
- Read/write spreadsheets
- Read/write cell values
- Run macros
- Format cells

In this chapter, we will use some of these actions to enhance the purchasing process to read off the shopping list from an Excel spreadsheet. We will start by importing the Excel VBO that contains the Blue Prism libraries that interact with Excel, following which we will use the Excel VBO to perform the following actions:

- Open, read, and close an Excel worksheet
- Write to a cell in the worksheet

Finally, **comma separated values** (**CSV**) files are often used in place of Excel to hold data. We will finish off the chapter by applying the same concepts we used for Excel to a CSV file.

Reading the shopping list from Microsoft Excel

As the hands-on tutorial for this chapter, we will be reading the shopping list from a Microsoft Excel spreadsheet. Previously, we hardcoded the shopping list by entering the items that we want to purchase as initial values of a collection. We wouldn't want to do that every week; editing the collection requires the person updating the list to be proficient in Blue Prism. Instead, what happens in real life is that the list is maintained somewhere like a Microsoft Excel file as a worksheet. Excel makes it easy for anyone, even a novice computer user, to enter their shopping needs.

Before we start the chapter, let's observe the following steps to prepare our shopping list:

1. Create a new Excel named `ShoppingList_Henry.xlsx`: We added the name of the shopper (in our example, that's our friend, Henry) at the back. In this way, you can have separate lists, one for each shopper.
2. Rename `Sheet1` to `List`. Delete `Sheet2` and `Sheet3`.
3. Enter the shopping list as shown here. We have three columns: `Item Name`, `Status`, and `Remarks`. Add whatever you want to purchase as rows in the spreadsheet:

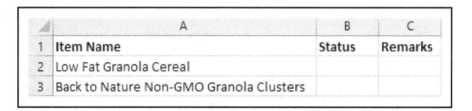

	A	B	C
1	Item Name	Status	Remarks
2	Low Fat Granola Cereal		
3	Back to Nature Non-GMO Granola Clusters		

4. Create a folder in the `C:\` drive. Name it `Shopping`. (Alternatively, you can create the folder anywhere you want; just remember its path.) The path to the file is now `C:\Shopping\ShoppingList_Henry.xlsx`. Save the shopping list Excel file in the folder.

Recall that in the earlier chapters, we simply added a note stage to the **Get list of items** page. In this chapter, we will fill it in with the actual steps to read the `ShoppingList_Henry.xlsx` Excel file and to update the status of each item as we go along.

Importing the Excel VBO

Before we make use of the Excel VBO library, check to see whether it has been installed in your environment. If not, add it in.

Here is how to import it:

1. From Blue Prism Studio, click **File** | **Import**.
2. The **Import Release** dialog opens. Click **Browse** to look for the file to be imported.
3. Navigate to `C:\Program Files\Blue Prism Limited\Blue Prism Automate\VBO`. All the libraries that ship with Blue Prism can be located in this folder.
4. Look for the file named `BPA Object - MS Excel.xml` and double-click on it to open it.
5. The file gets imported to the database. Click **Finish** when done. The MS Excel VBO Object now shows up in the list, as shown here:

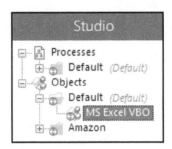

Using MS Excel VBO to open, show, and close Microsoft Excel

Let's dive into the action by starting up Excel with the MS Excel VBO library. Here, we are going to fire up the Microsoft Excel application and make it visible by showing it on the screen. Finally, to keep the desktop clean, we shall close the application gracefully.

Before we begin

Before we start building the process, we will observe the following steps to remove the stubs that we placed on the page earlier:

1. Open the `Weekly purchase of groceries` process for editing.
2. Click on the **Get list of items to purchase** page.
3. Delete the note stage that we added as placeholders for the actual steps so that there is nothing between the **Start** and **End** stages.
4. In the **Output - List of Items to Purchase** collection properties dialog, click on the **Fields** tab. Remove all the fields by clicking on the **Clear Fields** button. This will also remove all the initial values that we entered previously.

The starting point for the **Get list of items to purchase** page should resemble the following diagram:

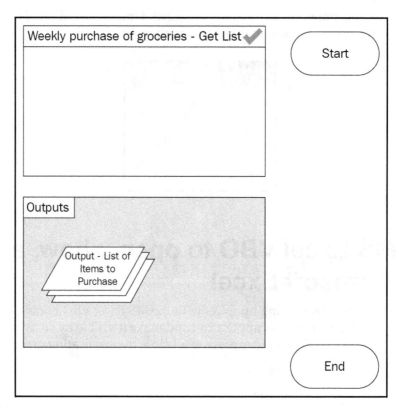

Opening Excel

Now that we have cleaned up the canvas, let's proceed to use the MS Excel VBO to open an instance of Excel, as shown in the following steps:

1. Drag an **Action** stage from the toolbox and drop it beneath the **Start** stage. Assign the **Action** stage the following property values:
   - **Name**: `Create Excel instance`
   - **Business Object**: `MS Excel VBO`
   - **Action**: `Create instance`

2. In the properties dialog, click on the **Outputs** tab. Notice that there is an output field named **handle**. In the **Store In** field, click on the **Data Item** icon to create a new data item with the name **handle**. Close the dialog. The handle data item is a number that uniquely identifies the instance of Excel that is opened. Windows is capable of opening multiple instances of Excel at any one time. We will use the handle to keep track of which particular Excel window we are working with.

3. Next, we will make Excel visible on the screen by showing it. Add another **Action** stage beneath the **Create Excel instance** stage. Assign it the following property values:
   - **Name**: `Show`
   - **Business Object**: `MS Excel VBO`
   - **Action**: `Show`

4. In the **Inputs** tab, drag and drop the **handle** data item into the **Value** field of the **handle** input.

5. Link all the stages together. The completed diagram is shown as follows:

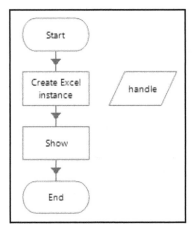

Closing Excel

After opening and showing Excel, let's close it (I know it sounds lame to close it so soon after opening Excel, but bear with me for now; we shall do the interesting stuff, such as reading the Excel file into a collection, in a short while):

1. Drag another **Action** stage and drop it beneath the **Show** Stage. Assign it the following property values:
   - **Name:** Close Instance
   - **Business Object:** MS Excel VBO
   - **Action:** Close Instance

2. Notice that the **Inputs** section contains two fields: **handle** and **Save Changes**. In the **handle** input field, drag and drop the **handle** data item. The **Save Changes** field gives us the option to save any changes that may have been made to the Excel file. Since we didn't make any updates to the spreadsheet, leave the **Save Changes** value as **False**.

3. Back on the canvas, link all the stages together so that the completed diagram appears as follows:

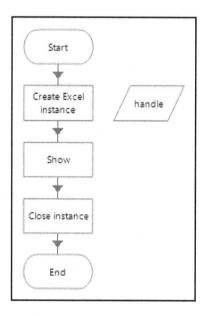

Run the process. See that Excel gets started, appears on the screen briefly, and closes soon after. At this point, we have not done anything, not even open a file. We will do that in just a bit.

What is the MS Excel VBO made up of?

What is inside the MS Excel VBO library? Let's take a look at what it contains. From Object Studio, double-click on **MS Excel VBO** and open it for editing (alternatively, right-click on the **Create Excel instance** action that we added earlier and select **View action in Object Studio**).

Click on the little arrow at the side of the **Initialise** tab ▼ 🔗 Initialise . The list of MS Excel VBO actions is extensive and contains many ready-to-use actions. Let's take a close look at one of the actions. Choose the **Create Instance** action that we used just a moment ago. Earlier, we saw that the **Create Instance** action starts the Microsoft Excel application. How does it do it? Notice that the action contains a code block. Double-click on the **Create Instance** code block and click on the **Code** tab.

There are just three lines of working code, as shown in the following screenshot. Simply put, the Excel VBO object uses code to trigger the Excel application:

```
Inputs  Outputs  Code

1
2    Dim excel as Object = CreateObject("Excel.Application")
3
4    ' Create a GUID with which we can kill the instance later
5    ' if we have to play hardball to get rid of it.
6    excel.Caption = System.Guid.NewGuid().ToString().ToUpper()
7
8    handle = GetHandle(excel)
```

What is Microsoft Excel VBA?

The code that the MS Excel VBO uses to operate Excel is a programming language called **Visual Basic for Applications** (VBA). The language has its roots way back in the day when Visual Basic (the original version before ASP.NET came into the picture) was in its heyday.

While Visual Basic has since been superseded by Visual Basic.NET, VBA still lives on. It has been embedded in many Office applications, Excel and Word included, as a power tool for us to get more out of the application than what is available out of the box. We use VBA to write macros, perform complex calculations, and to execute simple programming tasks, such as connecting to an external data store to download data into a spreadsheet.

The nice thing about VBA is that it allows Blue Prism to work with Excel programmatically. In this way, it provides a very stable way for the robot to read and write data back to Excel. It will not be affected by whether or not the buttons shift position, or if there are any new add-ins installed and such like.

We won't be covering the nuts and bolts of Excel VBA programming in this book. For a getting started guide, refer to MSDN (`https://msdn.microsoft.com/en-us/vba/office-shared-vba/articles/getting-started-with-vba-in-office`).

Opening an Excel file

We have fired up Excel, but we have yet to open the **ShoppingList_Henry.xlsx** file. Let's get to it now by observing the following steps:

1. With the **Get List of items to purchase** page opened, drag an **Action** stage and drop it beneath the **Show** stage. Configure it as follows:
    - **Name**: Open List
    - **Business Object**: MS Excel VBO
    - **Action**: Open Workbook

2. In the **Inputs** tab of the **Open List** stage, the action is expecting two inputs: **handle** and **File name**.
    - In the **handle** field: Drag the **handle** data item that was created when we created an instance of Excel in the **handle** field.
    - In the **File Name** field: Drag the **Shopping List Excel File Path** data item that we created earlier to contain the file path to the Excel file (which contains the actual path, C:\Shopping\ShoppingList_Henry.xlsx).

3. Click **Outputs**. In **Workbook Name**, click on the **Data item** icon to automatically create a data item with the name **Workbook Name**.

4. Link the stages together, as shown in the following diagram:

Now, when you run the process, it not only fires up Excel, but it also opens up our shopping list spreadsheet. It's still not doing very much. What we really want it to do is to read the data in the spreadsheet and put all that data into a collection for the robot to work with.

Reading an entire worksheet into a collection

Now that we have the Excel worksheet opened, we can instruct the robot to read its contents. If you look at the list of available actions in the MS Excel VBO library, you will see the following possible actions to choose from:

- **Get worksheet as collection**: Reads everything from cell A1 to the last populated row and column.

- **Get worksheet as collection offset**: Reads everything from a specified cell to the last populated row and column.
- **Get worksheet range as collection**: Reads everything from the specified start cell to the specified end cell.
- **Get worksheet as collection (Fast)**: This action has been deprecated. It is still in the list for backward compatibility reasons.

The action that you select depends on how your spreadsheet is formatted. Since our shopping list starts from cell A1, we will use Get worksheet as collection.

1. Drag an **Action** stage and drop it beneath the **Open List** stage. Configure it to have the following property values:
   - **Name**: `Read worksheet`
   - **Business Object**: `MS Excel VBO`
   - **Action**: `Get Worksheet As Collection`
2. The **Inputs** panel of the **Read worksheet** properties dialog expects three input fields to be filled in:
   - Handle: Drag and drop **[handle]** from **Data Explorer**
   - **Workbook Name**: Drag and drop **[Workbook Name]** from Data Explorer
   - **WorksheetName**: Enter the name of the worksheet to read. In our case, the worksheet name is `"List"`. Remember the double quotes!
3. Click **Outputs**. We want to store the contents of the Excel in the collection named **Output – List of Items to Purchase**. Drag the collection and drop it in the output field named **Data**.
4. Now, link the stages together, as shown in the following diagram:

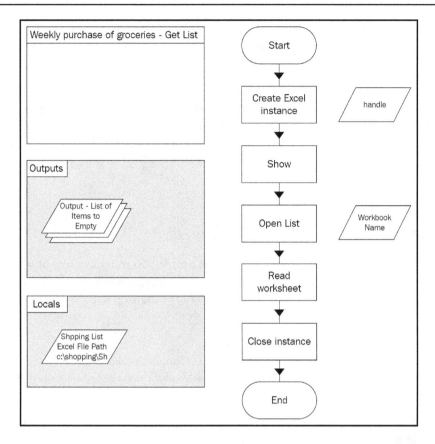

Run the process again. This time, the contents of the shopping list spreadsheet get populated into the **Output – List of Items to Purchase** collection. Open up the collection and check its current values. The first row of the worksheet automatically becomes the header of the collection. The data gets populated into the collection in the exact way it was entered in the spreadsheet, as shown in the following screenshot:

Fields	Initial Values	Current Values		
Item Name (Text)			Status (Text)	Remarks (Text)
Low Fat Granola Cereal				
Back to Nature Non-GMO Granola Clusters				

It is also possible to write back the collection to the Excel spreadsheet using the **Write Collection** action. Give it a try as an exercise on your own.

 Sometimes, an Excel worksheet may contain blank rows. These empty rows will be read into the collection and may cause exceptions when we try to process the data. To remove empty rows, use the **Remove Empty Rows** action found in the **Utility - Collection Manipulation** Business Object.

Writing to a cell

Look at the shopping list spreadsheet. The **Status** and the **Remarks** columns are currently empty. You may have guessed it by now, but those empty spaces are meant to be used by the robot to indicate whether or not it was successful in making the purchase. If, for some reason, it encountered an error while adding the item to the cart, it will write something into the remarks column.

Earlier, we read the entire spreadsheet into a collection. Now, let's try to update it using the MS Excel VBO library. To do so, we will create a new action page, as shown in the following steps:

1. In the **Weekly purchase of groceries** process, create a new page named **Update Status**.

2. Add two inputs to the **Start** stage. We want to pass in the status text message as well as the row number to update. Add the following input fields:

Name	Data type
Status	Text
Row Number	Number

For each of the input fields, click on the **Data Item** icon in the **Store In** field to automatically create them.

3. Repeat the steps to create an Excel instance, then show and open the workbook, and close the instance. As a shortcut, you can copy these steps from the **Get list of items to purchase** page. Here's how the diagram should appear once it's completed:

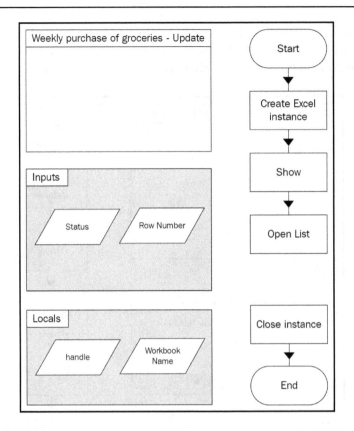

4. Drag another **Action** stage and drop it beneath **Open List**. Set the following property values:
   - **Name**: Update Status
   - **Business Object**: MS Excel VBO
   - **Action**: Set Cell Value

5. Notice that the **Set Cell Value** action expects three input values:
   - **Handle**: Drag and drop [handle] from **Data Explorer**.
   - **Cell Reference**: It's expecting the actual cell reference number. In our Shopping list file, the Status column is B. Insert the following formula: "B" & [Row Number] + 1. We get the row number from the input data item, **[Row Number]**. The formula adds 1 to the number since the first row is always the header.
   - **Value**: Drag and drop **[Status]** from **Data Explorer**. This is another item that is obtained as an input.

6. After we have updated the Excel file, we want to save the changes. Double-click on the **Close instance** stage and change the **Save Changes** input value to **True**.

7. Finally, link all the stages together. The completed diagram looks as follows:

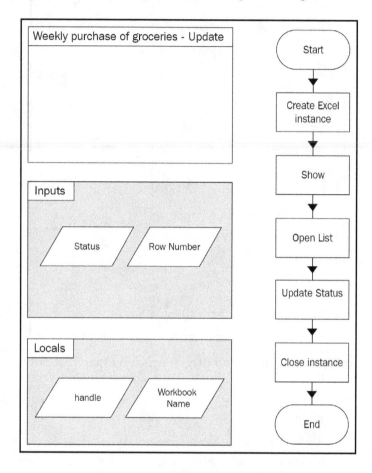

In the same way that we write text to a single cell, we can also choose to read a cell value into a text data item. To do so, use the **Get Cell Value** action. Just specify the handle and the name of the cell that you want to read from (for example, B2).

We aren't done yet. We still need to call the Update Status page each time we complete adding an item to the cart. Let's go back to the **Search and Add Item to Cart** page and add the following stages:

1. Open the **Search and Add Item to Cart** page. Add a **Data Item** to the page to store the status value.
   - **Name:** Status
   - **Data Type:** Text

2. Add another **Data Item** to store the row number:
   - **Name:** Row number
   - **Data Type:** Number
   - **Initial Value:** 1

3. Now complete the diagram by adding new stages beneath the **Close Amazon** stage, as shown in the following diagram:

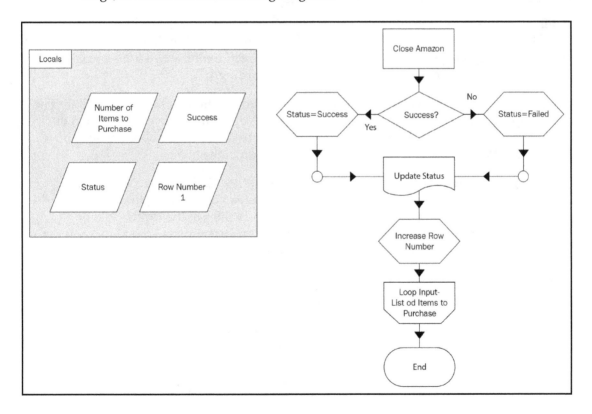

Use the following table to configure each new stage:

Stage name	Stage type	Property	Value
Success?	Decision	Expression	[Success]
Status=Success	Calculation	Expression	"Successfully added item to the cart"
		Store Result In	Status
Status=Failed	Calculation	Expression	"Failed to add item to cart"
		Store Result In	Status
Update Status	Page	Page	Update Status
		Status	[Status]
		Row Number	[Row Number]
Increase Row Number	Calculation	Expression	[Row Number]+1
		Store Result In	Row Number

After attempting to add the item to the cart, we check whether or not the item has been added successfully by examining the **Success** data item. We set the **Status** message and use the **Update Status** page to update the Excel spreadsheet. Finally, as we process each row in our to-do list, we will increase the **Row Number** accordingly.

Try running the process. Each time the robot tries to add an item to the cart, it will update the shopping list with the status if it was successful. Note that we have not handled the unhappy cases. If there is an error in adding the item to the cart, the robot will terminate the process. We will get to handling exceptions later on in the book.

Alternatively, we could have used the **Write Collection** action of the MS Excel VBO object to do the same job. Instead of updating the Excel spreadsheet directly, we first update the values in the **Input - List of Items to Purchase** collection. When we have completed the loop, we write the entire collection back to the Excel spreadsheet.

Considerations for comma separated values (CSV)

There is a special type of spreadsheet known as a CSV. This is short for Comma Separated Values, which is a fancy way of calling a row that has values delimited by commas.

An example of such a row is the following:

ID	Title
1	Don't be Horrid Henry
2	Horrid Henry and the Fangmangler

It really isn't much to look at visually. It actually appears as one clump of text, which makes reading it rather hard to do. However, in many systems that integrate with other third-party systems that do not have Microsoft Excel installed, CSV is a good alternative for storing tabular data.

Blue Prism has a couple of utilities that make it really easy to work with CSV files. They are stored in the following library files:

- Utility — Strings library
- Utility — File Management

We will try out the examples in the Utility - Strings library to see them in action. First, check to see whether you have imported both the Utility — Strings.xml and Utility — File Management.xml libraries. If not, observe the steps in the section "Importing the Excel VBO" to import these libraries into Blue Prism Studio.

Converting a collection to CSV

Suppose that we are working with a collection and we want to save it as a CSV file, what should we do? Let's dive right into the following steps to find out:

1. Create a new process. Name it **Trying out CSV**.
2. With the **Main** page opened, add a **Collection**. Give it the name **Favorite Books** and define the following two **Fields**:
   - ID (Number)
   - Title (Text)
3. Populate the **Initial Values** with a list of your favorite titles. An example is shown in the following table:

ID	Title
1	Don't be Horrid Henry
2	Horrid Henry and the Fangmangler

4. Drag an **Action** stage and drop it beneath the **Start** stage. Assign it the following property values:
   - **Name**: Get list as CSV
   - **Business Object**: Utility – Strings
   - **Action**: Get Collection as CSV
5. It expects only one input, which is the collection that we want to convert to CSV. In the **Input Collection** field, drag and drop **Favorite Books**. In the **Ouputs** tab, notice that it produces a single text value named **Collection CSV** that will contain the list in comma-separated-value format. Click on the **Data Item** icon to automatically create the **Collection CSV** data item.
6. Back on the **Main** page, link all the stages together as follows:

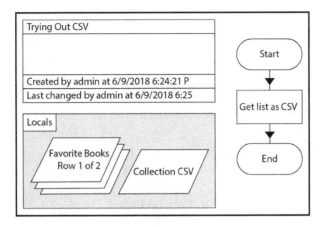

Run the process. When it reaches the end, check what is stored in the **Current Value** of **Collection CSV**. Did you manage to get the same collection, but this time tabulated as a CSV, as shown here? Take a look at the following screenshot:

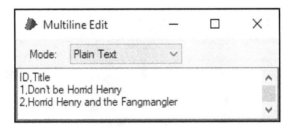

 After getting the collection as CSV, a logical next step would be to save it to a file. Try it yourself using the **Write Text File** action of the **Utility – File Management** object.

Converting a CSV to a collection

Now, let's try the reverse. We have converted a collection to a CSV, so what about transforming a CSV back into a collection? Observe the following steps to see how it's done:

1. With the **Main** page opened, drag and drop another **Action** just above the **End** stage and configure it as follows:
   - **Name**: Convert CSV back to collection
   - **Business Object**: Utility – Strings
   - **Action**: Get CSV As Collection

2. The **Inputs** tab expects the following three given things:
   - **CSV**: Drag and drop **Collection CSV** from **Data Explorer**.
   - **First Row is Header:** Set the value to be `True`. We want to use the first row to name the columns of the collection.
   - **Schema**: Leave it blank. If the first row is not to be the header, you have the option of passing in another collection that contains the header names.

3. In the **Outputs** tab, we specify the collection that we want to store the converted list in. Click on the **Data Item** icon to create a collection with the name **Output Collection**.

4. Link the process from **Start** to **End,** including the new **Action** stage, as shown here:

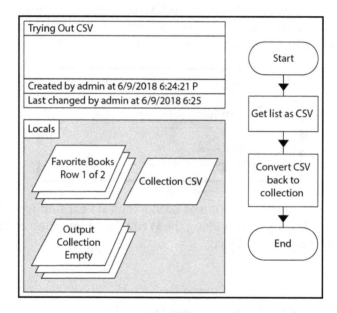

Now, run the process. When it completes, check the current value of **Output Collection**. Observe that the CSV rows have been successfully converted back into a collection, as shown in the following screenshot:

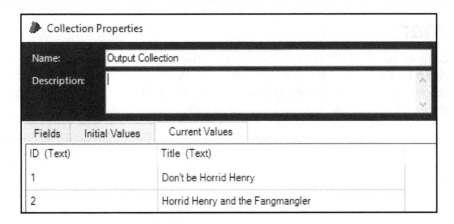

 Usually, the CSVs that we work with are stored in files. There is an action named **Get CSV Text As Collection** in the **Utility - File Management** object that gives the convenience of reading a CSV file directly into a collection.

Using the MS Excel VBO with CSV files

Microsoft Excel also supports CSV files. Therefore, you can use the same techniques that we covered in the first part of the chapter to work with CSV files, with a little tweak. Each time you attempt to open or save a CSV, you may get prompts, such as the following:

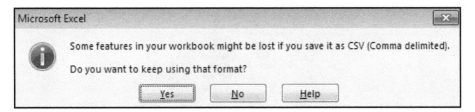

To suppress them, just don't include the **Show** stage when working with CSV files. The downside is that you won't get to see the Excel file on the screen as the robot runs.

Summary

We have covered one of the most common applications that Blue Prism processes have to interact with on a day-to-day basis: Microsoft Excel. We have seen how to open an Excel file, read its contents to a collection, and write to a cell. In addition, we looked at a type of file known as a CSV, and saw how to read it as a collection and vice versa.

In the next chapter, we will train the robot to send and receive email using Microsoft Outlook.

Sending and Receiving Emails $\boldsymbol{9}$

Reading emails has become a large part of our everyday lives. The first thing we do in the morning when we reach the office is fire up Outlook to catch up on what has happened while we were away. Since robots model the way we work, the same can be said of them. The processes that robots execute often use email to do the following:

- Send status notifications when a process completes
- Send error messages when something goes wrong and requires human inspection
- Receive email orders to start a process

These are just some examples. There are many other areas where email has an important role in the processes that robots run.

In this chapter, we will learn the basics on how to configure the robot to do the following:

- Send emails
- Format the mail message body
- Send attachments
- Receive emails

Using the MS Outlook VBO to manage emails

Blue Prism has developed the MS Outlook VBO just for managing emails. It became available in August 2018 alongside the release of Blue Prism v6.3.

Before you can begin using the MS Outlook VBO, ensure that you have the following prerequisites installed:

- **Outlook automation**: This is a software component that was included in the Blue Prism installation file. Re-run the Blue Prism setup if you need to re-install this component.
- **Microsoft Outlook 2016**: It can be connected to Exchange or Gmail or Outlook.com. Your email provider doesn't matter, you just have to make sure that you are able to launch and open Outlook with a valid email address.
- **MS Outlook VBO**: Use the same steps as what we did earlier for the MS Excel.vbo file to import the MS Outlook VBO.xml file into Object Studio.

In earlier versions of Blue Prism, you had to install a separate utility, called MAPIEx, alongside a Blue Prism MAPIEx VBO. If you are working with an older version of Blue Prism that still requires the use of MAPIEx, do refer to the documentation available on the Blue Prism Portal for instructions on how to use it.

Sending emails

One of the most common actions that we perform with emails is to send them. Thankfully, the MS Outlook VBO makes it really easy to do so. In the purchasing process that we have been working on so far, the last step of the process is to email the requester when the items have been successfully added to the cart. They can then log into the Amazon.com site to review the items and pay for them to be delivered. Let's perform the following steps to get the robot to send out the email.

1. Open the **Weekly purchase of groceries** process. Edit the **Send Email Notification** page.
2. Drag an **Action** and place it just before the **End** stage. Assign it the following property values:
   - **Name**: Send Email to Requester
   - **Business Object**: MS Outlook VBO
   - **Action**: Send Email

If you imported the MS Outlook VBO file while the process was opened, you will have to close and re-open the process for the newly-imported Business Object to be available in the dropdown.

3. Take a look at the `Input` panel. The send email action expects input. Fill it up as follows:
   - **To**: Earlier, we prepared the email address of the requester. Drag and drop the **Email Address** data item.
   - **CC**: This is for email addresses we want to carbon copy the email to. Leave it blank.
   - **BCC**: This is for putting in email addresses we want to blind carbon copy the email to. Leave it blank.
   - **Subject**: `Your items have been added to the cart.`
   - **Message**: Drag and drop the **Email Message** data item.
   - **Attachments**: This is for adding attachments to go along with the email. Leave it blank for now.

4. Earlier, we specified the name of the requester in the Excel shopping list. For example, `c:\shopping\ShoppingList_Henry.xlsx` is Henry's shopping list. We need to extract the requester's name in order to figure out which address to send the email to. Add another **Action** stage directly below **Start**.

5. Assign it the following property values:
   - **Name**: `Get Requester`
   - **Expression**: `Replace(Right([Shopping List Excel File Path], Len([Shopping List Excel File Path])- InStr([Shopping List Excel File Path], "_")), ".xlsx", "")`
   - **Store Result In**: `Requester`

In the expression, we have put in a formula to extract out the requester name that is between the underscore (_) and the `.xlsx` file extension.

6. Back on the canvas, link up the diagram such that it appears as follows:

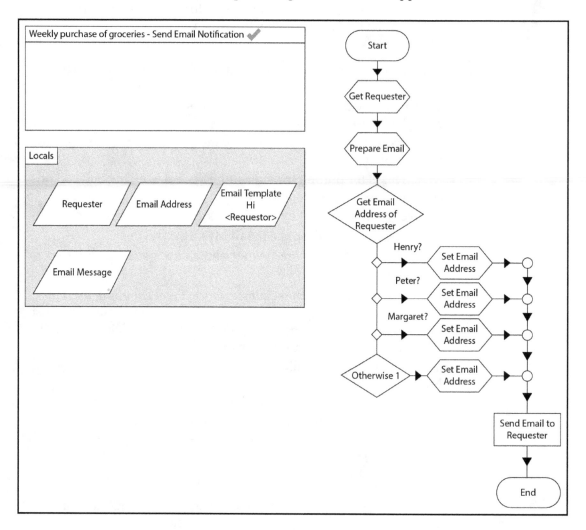

7. Before we send any email, it's best to just check that it will go to an account that you have access to. We don't want to unwittingly send out test email messages to complete strangers. Click on all the **Set Email Address** stages and change the email specified in the expression to one that you can access.

Run the process from start to finish. While the process is running, Outlook opens for a short while before closing again while the robot sends out the emails. After the process completes its run, open Outlook again and check the "Sent" folder to see the actual email that was sent out. If you have access to the recipient's email address, take a look at their mailboxes and look for the email. Did you get the email?

Formatting emails

Take a good look at the email that was sent out. Although we formatted it to have proper line breaks, somehow Outlook flattened the format of the message into a single line, like the following:

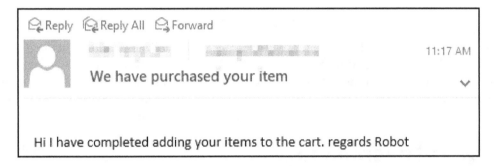

To format the email message properly, we will have to make use of HTML. Here's what we originally put in the email template data item:

```
Hi <Requester>
I have completed adding your items to the cart.

Regards
 Robot
```

We will use the paragraph tag (<p></p>) as well as the line break tag (<br/>) to format the message nicely into paragraphs. Replace the **Initial Value** stored in the **Email Template** data item with the following HTML code:

```
<html><body>
 <p>Hi <Requester></p>
 <p>I have completed adding your items to the cart.</p>
 <p>regards<br />Robot</p>
 </body></html>
```

Now run the process again. The email that is sent out is now nicely formatted:

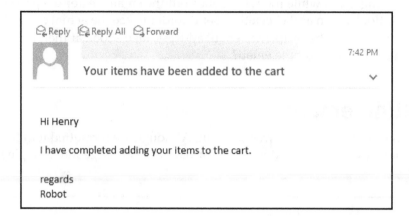

With HTML, you can do a lot more than add paragraphs and line breaks. You can format text to be bolded, italicized, underlined, or in different colors. It is also possible to do more complex stuff, such as adding in an entire table. There are many online resources that teach the basics of HTML. One such site is the HTML Primer.

Sending attachments

The **Send Email** action has an input parameter for **Attachments**. It was expecting the list of files we wanted to send along with the email to be separated by commas. Earlier, we left it blank. Let's see what happens when we send back the Excel that was used to place the order. Follow these steps:

1. On the **Send Email Notification page**, double-click on the **Send Email** stage to open its properties dialog.
2. Drag and drop the **Shopping List Exce**l File Path data item into the **Attachments** field. Close the dialog and run the process again. This time the Excel file is sent as an attachment along with the email.

When you are done, save and close the **Weekly purchase of groceries** process.

You can send multiple attachments by separating their paths using a comma; for example, `c:\File1.docx, c:\File2.pptx`.

Receiving emails

The next most common activity that robots do with emails is receive them. Emails are often the starting point of many processes, and the following list provides some examples:

- Reports received by email are to be scrubbed, processed, and filed
- Orders received by email require data-entry into another system

This is why Blue Prism has provided not just one, but at least three different actions for searching email in the Inbox:

- **Get Received Items (Basic)**: This is the easiest to use. It covers the simplest scenarios, where you just want to look for emails based on the common search criteria such as sender name, sender email, received date, subject, and message.
- **Get Received Items (Advanced):** This expects you to provide a search filter in the form of a text string. You need to understand how to build the query before using this action.
- **Get Received Items (Expert)**: This is the most complex to use as you need to understand the DASL, which is a special syntax for working with the Outlook search filter.

The MS Outlook VBO also offers similar actions for searching the Sent folder.

Basic

Let's start by getting the robot to look for emails in our mailbox using the Basic method. The following steps describe how to create a brand new process to see how the action works:

1. Create a new process in Blue Prism Studio named **Receive Emails**.
2. In the Main page, drag and drop an Action stage and place it between the Start and End stages. Configure it as follows:
   - **Name**: Search for emails
   - **Business Object**: MS Outlook Email VBO
   - **Action**: Get Received Item (Basic)

3. Take a look at the list of **Inputs**. None of them are mandatory. If you choose to leave all the input blank, the action will attempt to get all the mail items in your inbox. Unless you have kept your inbox really clean, chances are it will take some time before you get back the results. Usually, we will search with some criteria in mind.

The options available in **Basic** mode are:

- **Subfolder**: By default, the search covers the Inbox and all its subfolders. However, you can restrict the search to be within a specific subfolder by putting in its path here; for example, `Inbox\Folder A`.
- **Sender name**: If you are looking for an email from someone, enter the sender's display name here, for example `John Doe`.
- **Sender email**: To be more accurate, you may choose to enter the sender's email address instead. This will avoid any confusions with names that look the same, such as `john.doe@anonymous.com`.
- **Received earliest**: Gives you the option to restrict the search to retrieve all emails received no earlier than a specified date and time. For example, putting in a date of `01/01/2018 00:00` will get all emails received after January, 1st 2018.
- **Received Latest**: On the flip side, this gives you the option of restricting the search to only get emails received no later than the specified date and time. For example, if the received latest date is `31/03/2018 23:59`, we will get all the emails sent before `31 Mar 2018 23:59`. **Received Latest** and **Received Earliest** are often used together to search within a slice of time.
- **Subject**: Search for emails with specific text in the subject field. Note that searches by subject are exact matches unless you use a wildcard. If you want to look for all messages with the word **deals** in the subject line, enter `*deals*`.
- **Message**: Similar to using the subject filter, but it looks for the text in the message body instead.
- **Include Read**: Includes emails that have been marked as read in the search results. If left blank, the search will include emails that have been read.
- **Include Unread**: Includes emails that have been marked as unread in the search results. If left blank, the search will include unread emails.

4. Give it a try. Configure the action to look for the email that we just sent in the earlier part of the chapter. Apply the following search criteria:

   - **Subject**: We fixed the subject of the email that was sent out. To apply it back here, enter `Your items have been added to the cart.`

   - **Received earliest**: To search only for email received today, enter `Today()`.

To limit the search to only unread mail, set the Include Unread flag to `False`.

5. Switch to the **Outputs** tab. There are two results that are returned by the **Get Receive Items (Basic)** action. Click on the **Data Item** icon for both output to create them.

   - **Items** is a collection that holds the list of emails that matches the search criteria.

   - **Item Count** tells us how many items have been found.

6. Close any opened dialog screens. Back on the canvas, link up the diagram as follows:

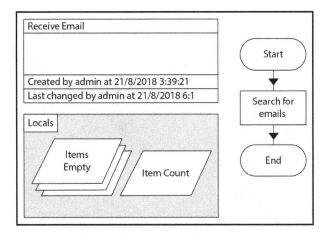

Run the process. When it completes, check the results by looking at the **Items** and **Item Count** data items. Did you manage to retrieve the email that we sent out earlier? If you open up **Items** and look at its **Current Values**, you will find the contents of the email. You can use a loop to iterate through the collection and read all the property values.

Play around with the action by setting other search criteria and see whether you are able to retrieve them from your inbox. For example, you may want to search for all emails with deals in the subject sent within the month of May, or for all emails from your favorite subscription sent in the past one year.

Advanced

Now let's perform the following steps to use the **Get Received Items (Advanced)** action to perform the same search that we did earlier:

1. In the **Main** action page of the **Receive Emails** process, double-click on the **Search for Emails** action. Change the **Action** to **Get Received Items (Advanced)**.
2. Notice that the **Inputs** are different. It now only expects two inputs:
   - **Subfolder**: Same as before, we can restrict the search to within a specified subfolder.
   - **Filter Expression**: Contains a single text string that we will use to formulate the search query.

We want to search for emails with the `"Your items have been added to the cart"` subject and received today. The filter expression is as follows:

```
"[subject] = 'Your Items have been added to the cart' And [SentOn]>='"
& Today() & "'"
```

Run the process. Did you manage to pull out the correct set of emails?

When do we use the Advance method? The Basic method will suffice for most of the cases that we encounter. However, the Basic method is restricted to a fixed set of search criteria. If we need to, say, search for email based on other properties, such as Size or `SentOnBehalfName`, we will need to use the Advanced method.

The easiest way to figure out how to build the Filter Expression is to use Outlook itself. From the Outlook ribbon, click **Home | Filter Email** (it's in the **Find** category). Use the **Search Tool** to build up the query that you need.

Expert

Finally, the following steps show how use the Get Received Items (Expert) to perform the same search:

1. Change the **Action** used in the **Search for emails** stage to **Get Received Items (Expert)**.
2. The list of input has changed again. This time, it has the following input:
   - **Subfolder**: Works the same way as the other two actions by restricting the query to a specific subfolder
   - **DASL query**: Instead of a filter expression, it's asking for a full query string

DASL (short for **DAV Searching and Locating**) is the Outlook search filter syntax. For the purpose of our example, the DASL query that we are looking for is as follows:

```
"@SQL=(""http://schemas.microsoft.com/mapi/proptag/0x0037001f"" LIKE
'%Your Items have been added to the cart%' AND
%today(""urn:schemas:httpmail:datereceived"")%)"
```

That query looks a lot more complicated than the one we used in **Advanced mode**. However, it is a lot more powerful. You can perform wildcard-matching, mix and match just about any property that is available in Outlook, and do many more complicated searches than possible with the other methods.

The trick to getting the DASL Query is to use the **Filter** function in Outlook. Right-click anywhere on a blank spot on the Ribbon bar in Outlook and choose to **Customize the Ribbon**. Look at **All Commands** and choose to add a **Filter....** Once you have added the **Filter** button, click on it from the Ribbon to open its dialog. Notice that the first three tabs, **Messages**, **More Choices**, and **Advanced**, are used to formulate the query.

For example, in our case, our filter looks as follows:

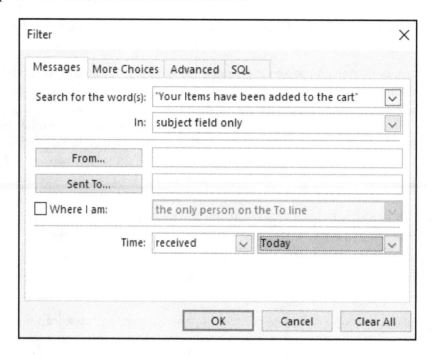

When you are done filling in the filter criteria, click on the **SQL** tab. Check the **Edit these criteria directly** box and copy out the query. Before we can use it, we need to make a few tweaks. For example, if our query
is `"http://schemas.microsoft.com/mapi/proptag/0x0037001f" LIKE '%my keyword%'` (which searches for all mail items with `my keyword` in the subject).

1. Prepend `@SQL=` in front of the query.
   The query becomes
   `@SQL="http://schemas.microsoft.com/mapi/proptag/0x0037001f" LIKE '%my keyword%'`.

2. Escape single double-quotes by using two double-quotes instead.
   The query
   becomes `@SQL=""http://schemas.microsoft.com/mapi/proptag/0x0037001f"" LIKE '%my keyword%'`.

3. Wrap the entire string with starting and closing double-quotes.
   The query becomes
   `"@SQL=""http://schemas.microsoft.com/mapi/proptag/0x0037001f"" LIKE '%my keyword%'"`.

There are also many resources on the internet that teach how to build the DASL query from scratch.

Summary

The MS Outlook VBO is a fairly new object that was made available to Blue Prism 6.3 developers. It has significantly simplified the task of sending and receiving emails compared to earlier versions. In this chapter, we completed the building of the purchasing process by getting the robot to send an email to the requester when the items have been added to the cart. We also explored the options for receiving emails. We saw that after the search is complete, the email properties, message body, and attachments are all stored into a collection that we can retrieve by looping.

In the next chapter, we will explore a topic that is very central to programming with Blue Prism: Control Room and Work Queues.

10
Control Room and Work Queues

One of the biggest drivers of deploying a robotic process into the workforce is to eliminate or at least minimize the need for human intervention. So far, each time we ran the process, we had to click on the **Play** button—that is an action that still requires a human. For the processes to be fully automated, robots should run them on their own, using a scheduler. In Blue Prism, all that action takes place in the control room. In this chapter, we will do the following:

- Explore the control room
- See how we can use the control room to get the robot to run on its own

The control room is also used for managing work queues. You could have a list of items in the work queue and a team of robots working on them at the same time. In this way, just like humans, it is possible for robots to work as a team.

We will learn how to do the following:

- Create a new work queue
- Add items to the queue
- Read from the queue
- Mark each item as completed (or not) when the robot is finished
- Filter for items in the work queue

Introducing the control room

We have been running processes by clicking on the **Run** button. It does a really neat job of showing us how the process moves through each stage. However, there is a problem with that approach; it still requires someone to click on it. In production mode, the process will be run by the robots unattended. To do so, we will use the control room. From Blue Prism Studio, click on the **Control** tab. The control room loads as shown in the following screenshot. By default, the main screen loaded is **Session Management**:

1. The left-hand panel lists all the sub-menus available in the control room. We will go through the main options in just a bit.
2. As this is the Session Management screen, we see on the right a list of the processes available. At this point, the list is empty.
3. We also see the list of all available resources (computers acting as robots) registered with the Blue Prism Server.
4. And, in the bottom panel, is the list of all processes that have run on which resources. Later on, we will see how we can use this section to start and stop processes:

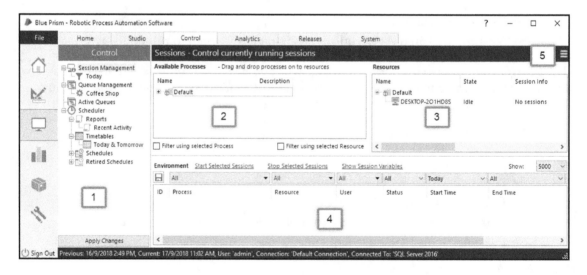

The control room is where process controllers will perform most of their work. It allows them to control the robots without having direct access to their screens. To understand what this means, let's run a process and watch the robots at work from the control room.

Process controllers are people who manage the processes and the robots they run on. They don't typically build the process (usually a developer does that). Instead, they are in charge of scheduling, monitoring the health of the process (whether it has completed successfully or terminated), and the workload on each robot. They are also the people who can manually trigger an ad hoc run of a process. In most enterprises, there is a need to separate the people who build/design the logic behind the process and the people who actually run it for security purposes. In this way, if a developer puts in malicious actions in a process, they can't run it on their own; they need to involve the process controllers. Blue Prism provides for this separation using the control room.

Publishing a process to the control room

Before a process can be run from the control room, it needs to be published. Observe the following steps to publish the **Weekly purchase of groceries** process:

1. Open the **Weekly purchase of groceries** process for editing. On the **Main** page, double-click on the **Page Information** box.
2. At the bottom of the dialog, check the **Publish this Process to Control Room** box.
3. Close the dialog and save the process.

Back in Studio, click on the **Control** tab. All the processes that are published are listed in the **Available Processes** panel, including the one that we have just published.

Running a process in the control room manually

Take a look at the **Resources** panel. It shows a list of all the runtime resources, also known as robots. If you are working in a lab environment, then you would probably only see one computer—the one that you are currently working on.

There are no resources in my list. My computer is not showing up. What should I do?

There is a setting to toggle whether or not the local computer also acts as a runtime resource. From Blue Prism Studio, click **System**. Then, in the **System** panel on the right, select **System | Settings**. In the **Settings** page, check the box **Start a personal Runtime Resource on this machine when users sign in to Blue Prism**.

We won't be covering the how-tos of setting up a runtime resource from the ground-up. The detailed steps of adding new robots to the list of resources can be found on the Blue Prism portal here: (https://portal. blueprism.com/system/files/documents/v6%20User%20Guide%20- %20Installing%20Enterprise%20Edition_1_1.pdf)

Let's see how we can run the process from the control room by observing the following steps:

1. Drag the **Weekly purchase of groceries** process from the list of **Available Processes** and drop it on top of the runtime resource that you want to run it on.
2. Look at the following panel. The process appears in orange with a status of **Pending**. This means that it is waiting to run. Right-click anywhere on the orange line and choose **Start**.

The process starts to run on its own. Note that the Status column says **Running** and the color of the line turns green. You should see the applications (Excel, Internet Explorer, and Outlook) that we have called from the process opening and closing as the robot interacts with them. Watch the robot run the process from start to finish. The following lists two possible outcomes reflected in the **Status** column:

- **Completed**: The color of the line is black. The process has successfully completed.
- **Terminated**: The color of the line is red. The robot encountered an error while running the process.

Don't worry if the process terminated. We will cover how to troubleshoot and handle exceptions in the next chapter.

While the process is running, keep your hands off the mouse and keyboard. The robot will be moving the mouse and pressing keys. If you interfere with its operation, the process may get interrupted with errors.

Scheduling processes

It was great to see Blue Prism running the process from the control room. However, we have merely replaced clicking **Run** with dragging and dropping. To truly automate the execution of the process, we use the scheduler. The following steps use the scheduler to schedule the process to run on its own.

1. Look at the **Control** panel on the right. Right-click on **Schedules** and select **New Schedule**.

2. Give the schedule a meaningful name; for example, **One time run - Weekly purchase of groceries**. You give the schedule any name you deem fit. We've added the planned run day and process name in the schedule's name so that it's easy to pick out what the scheduled run is going to do and when.

3. In the **Schedule** section, you can choose the frequency of the run and which day and time you want the process to start. We shall go with a one-time run two minutes from now. Configure the schedule as follows:
   - **Runs**: Once
   - **Starts On**: Choose today's date and a time that is two minutes from now

4. There is an empty task created along with the new schedule. It shows up as a child item with a little blue dot on the side. Click on it and give it the name **Weekly purchase of groceries**. Drag the process from the list of **Available Processes** and drop it on the resource that we want to use on the right.

5. Click **Apply Changes** for the schedule to be saved.

And we have now finished. Leave the computer alone for a couple of minutes. Did the process start as scheduled? When the process completes, you can click on **Session Management** to see its status.

My process did not run as scheduled. Why?

If you are running Blue Prism as a laboratory, schedules will not get triggered. For schedules to work correctly, you will need to configure and start the Blue Prism Service on the application server.

In addition, a Blue Prism robot can only run one task at a time. If you have scheduled for the process to run while the robot is busy, it will not run.

What are work queues?

Earlier, we saw how a process can be assigned to run on a selected resource in the control room. What if the process is working on a very long to-do list that is taking the robot a long time to clear everything? There is a way to split up the work between multiple robots using work queues.

Imagine going to your favorite coffee shop to order that morning cup of coffee. You step into the shop and see a long line of people waiting to place their order at the cashier. Thankfully, there are two cashiers open. The queue moves along twice as fast. Using the same analogy, you can add more robots to work on the same process to speed things up.

In this way, robots can work as a team. Let's see what a work queue looks like in Blue Prism by recreating the preceding coffee shop scenario.

Creating a work queue

Work queues are defined in the **System** tab of Blue Prism Studio. The following steps show how to create a new work queue:

1. From Blue Prism Studio, click **System**. From the left-hand panel, select **Workflow | Work Queues**.
2. The right-hand side shows the **Queue Details**. Configure it as follows:
   - **Name**: Coffee Shop
   - **Key Name**: ID
3. When done, click the **Apply** button. The queue is now ready to be used.

Adding items to the queue

We have created a queue but it does not have any items in it. We have a long list of thirsty people waiting to get their coffee. Let's use the following steps to put their orders into the queue by creating a process to simulate the cashiers who will take the orders.

1. Click on the **Studio** tab. Create a process named **Coffee Cashiers**.

2. Add a **Collection** to the page. Give it the name **Orders**. Configure it to have the following fields:
   - ID (number)
   - Item purchased (text)
   - Special request (text)

3. In the **Initial Values** tab, add items to the collection. Go ahead and fill it up with a list of your favorite drinks. Here's our list:

ID	Item purchased	Special request
1	Caramel Macchiato Frappuccino	
2	Flat White	Less sugar
3	English Breakfast Tea	Less sugar, with lemon

4. Drag an **Action** stage and drop it beneath **Start**. Assign its properties as follows:
   - **Name:** Add Orders to Queue
   - **Business Object:** Work Queues
   - **Action:** Add To Queue

5. The Add To Queue action expects a few inputs. Fill out the following:
   - **Queue Name:** "Coffee Shop"
   - **Data:** Drag and drop the Orders collection that we just created
   - **Status:** "Pending"

The completed diagram is shown here:

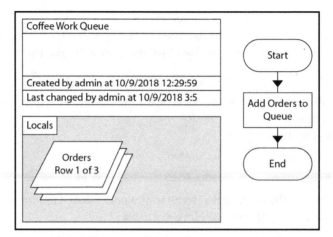

6. Run the process. When the process completes, go to the control room. Select **Queue Management | Coffee Shop**. The items have been added to the queue, as shown in the following screenshot:

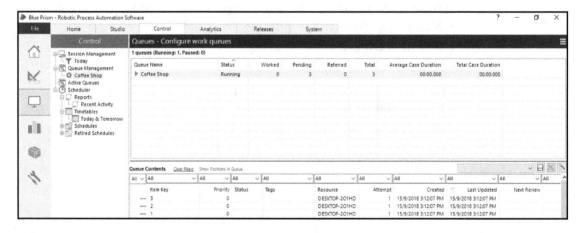

At this point, you can't see the details of the work items. All you get to see right now is the **Item Key** that stores the ID. You won't be able to tell which item is the coffee and which one is the tea. The details are stored in the work item and we will see how it is retrieved by the robot as it works through the queue in just a moment. In addition, the status of all the items is **Pending**, which is expected as we set "Pending" to be the default status of all newly added items to the queue.

Getting the next item in the queue

Now that we have some orders in the queue, we shall attend to them. Let's observe the following steps to create a process to simulate the baristas who will make and serve drinks:

1. Create a process and give it the name `Coffee Baristas`.
2. Drag an **Action** stage and drop it beneath **Start**. Configure it as follows:
   - **Name:** `Get next order`
   - **Business Object:** `Work Queues`
   - **Action:** `Get Next Item`
3. In the **Inputs** panel, fill in the queue that we want to pull the orders from:
   - **Queue Name:** `"Coffee Shop"`
4. The **Get Next Item** action creates a few outputs. Click on the **Outputs** tab and click on the **Data Item** icon for all the outputs to generate the corresponding item:
   - **Item ID**: The ID of the item that is currently being processed
   - **Data**: A collection that contains the full details of what the item is
   - **Status**: Tells us the status of the item and whether it is waiting to be processed, completed, or has an exception
   - Attempts: The number of attempts on the item
5. Link up all the stages so that it appears as follows:

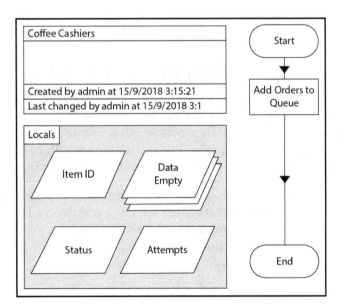

Run the process. Observe the following outputs after the process gets the next order:

- **Item ID** contains a long string of text known as a **GUID** (**Globally Unique Identifier**). It is used by Blue Prism to uniquely identify each item in the work queue.
- **Data** contains the details that we uploaded into the queue. The **ID**, **Item Name**, and **Special Request** are all stored here. We will use it later to process the drink order.
- **Status** shows **Pending** (remember this is the default that we put in for all new orders), which means that we have not yet processed this item.
- **Attempts** shows 0, as this is the first time we are processing this item

Go back to the control room and look at the **Coffee Shop** work queue. Notice that the item that was retrieved has a lock icon next to the **Item Key** column (see the following). This means that the robot that picked up the item has placed a lock on it. In this way, if you have multiple robots working on the same queue, they won't accidentally pick up the same item to process:

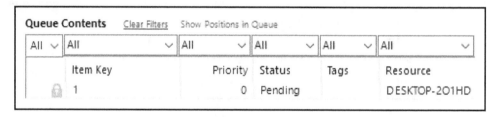

Checking for more items in the queue

After the process reaches the **End** stage, notice that it only managed to get one drink order. We have three drink orders; how do we get the remaining two? The trick is to call the **Get Next Item** action again. The **Get Next Item** action will continue to get the items in the queue until it reaches the end of the queue. When that happens, **Item ID** will contain an empty string. Let's use the following steps to put that logic into our flow diagram:

1. We want to check to see whether there are any more orders in the queue waiting to be processed by checking the **Item ID**. Drag and drop a **Decision** stage and place it beneath **Get next order**. Configure it as follows:
   - **Name**: More Items in the Queue?
   - **Expression**: [Item ID]<>""

2. Link the **Yes** path back to the **Get next order** stage and the **No** path to **End,** as shown in the following diagram:

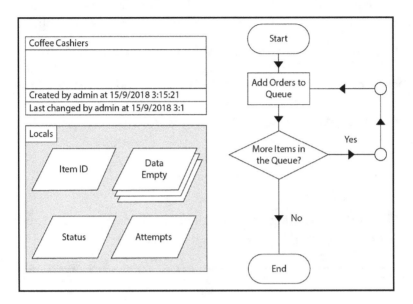

Use *F10* to step through the process. Notice that the **Item ID** changes each time the process gets the next order. Open up **Data** to check the details of the order. When it completes getting all the orders, the **Item ID** becomes blank and our process ends.

Go back to the control room and look at the items in the work queue. The lock has disappeared. In its place, we see purple flags (refer to the following screenshot). The flags indicate that something has gone wrong with that item and it requires manual intervention. The error message is shown in the **Tags** column and says **Automatically set exception at Cleanup**. What just happened? The exception occurred because getting the item and not doing anything about it is an exception. We need to process it and mark it as completed:

▷ 3	0	Exception: Automatically set exception at CleanUp
▷ 2	0	Exception: Automatically set exception at CleanUp
▷ 1	0	Exception: Automatically set exception at CleanUp

Marking the item as complete

For the item to be considered correctly processed, we should mark it as complete before moving on to the next item. Let's observe the following steps to modify the process again:

1. In the **Main** page of the **Coffee Cashiers** process, drag and drop a **Note** stage. Place it after the **Get next order** Stage. The note stage will simulate an actual process whereby a barista will make the drink and serve it to the customer. Set the `Note Text` to `Make and serve the drink`.

2. Next, drag an **Action** stage and place it after the **Note** stage. Configure it as follows:
   - **Name**: `Mark as complete`
   - **Business Object**: `Work Queues`
   - **Action**: `Mark Completed`

3. In the **Inputs** panel, drag and drop the **Item ID** data item into the **Item ID** field.

4. Save the process. The completed process looks as follows:

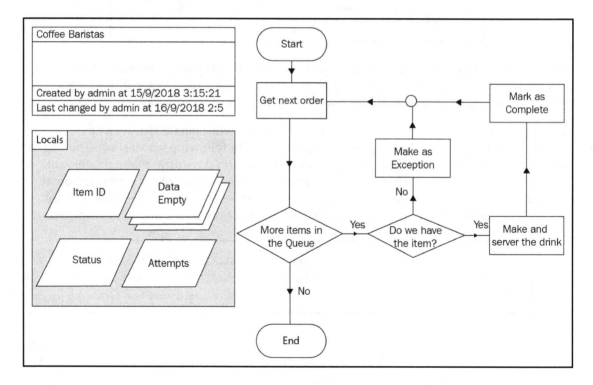

5. Rerun the coffee work queue process again to reload the items back into the queue. Go back to the control room and check that the new items are added to the queue.

Now, rerun the coffee cashiers process and observe that this time, the items are marked with a green check, as shown in the following screenshot. This indicates that they have been successfully processed and no further action is required:

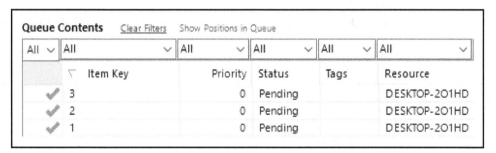

Updating the status

Did you notice something strange about the status of the work queue items when they have been marked as completed? You might have thought that the system should automatically change the status to completed, but no, they still show up as **Pending**. The reason is because we have to update the status ourselves using the **Update Status** action. Let's observe the following steps to update the order status:

1. In the **Main** page of the **Coffee Baristas** process, delete the note stage **Make and serve the drink**. We used it as a stub to represent making and serving the drink. Now, let's replace it with two more **Action** stages that update the status of the item to **Make Drink** and **Serve Drink** respectively. Add the action stages and configure them using the details provided in the following table:

	Action stage 1	Action stage 2
Name	Make Drink	Serve Drink
Business Object	Work Queues	
Action Status	Update Status	
Status	"Make Drink"	"Serve Drink"
Item ID	Drag and drop the **Item ID** data item from Data Explorer	

2. Drag an **Action** stage and drop it before the **Mark as complete** stage. Configure it as follows:
   - **Name**: Set status to Completed
   - **Business Object**: Work Queues
   - **Action**: Update Status

3. In the **Inputs**, set the following values:
   - **Status**: "Completed"
   - **Item ID**: Drag and drop the **Item ID** data item from **Data Explorer**

4. Link up all the stages as shown here:

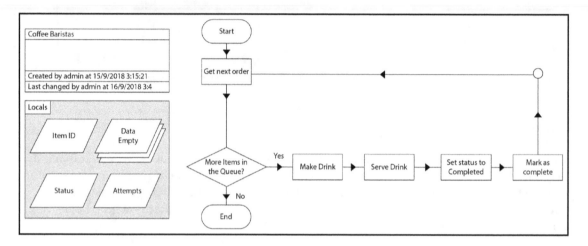

Reload the queue by running the **Coffee Cashiers** process. Then run the **Coffee Baristas** process one more time and observe that this time, all the items are completed and the status column is also updated to say **Completed**.

Marking the item as an exception

Well, not everything in the queue can be processed correctly. Even in a coffee shop, there will be cases where the drink does not make it to the customer. Reasons could be known or unknown. Common causes include running out of ingredients, lost orders, and so on. In the real world, there will be items that do not get completed. Let's simulate the case where the shop has run out of tea bags. Each time a customer orders tea, the item will be marked as an exception with the remarks **Item is out of stock**.

The following steps show how to do this:

1. In the **Coffee Baristas** process, drag a **Decision** stage and drop it after the **More Items in the Queue?** stage in the **Yes** path. Configure it as follows:
   - **Name:** `Do we have the item?`
   - **Expression:** `InStr([Data.Item Name],"Tea")=0`

   As long as the request is for tea, we will assume that it is out of stock. Of course, in a real-world application, you would be hooking up with an online inventory system to check whether there is stock of a particular item. For our particular exercise, we will just hardcode the check.

2. Drag an **Action** stage onto the diagram and drop it in the **No** path of the **Do we have the item?** stage. Assign it the following property values:
   - **Name:** `Mark as Exception`
   - **Business Object:** `Work Queues`
   - **Action:** `Mark Exception`

3. In the **Inputs** tab, fill in the following:
   - **Item ID**: Drag and drop the Item ID data item
   - **Exception Reason:** `Item is out of stock`

4. Link up the stages as shown in the following diagram:

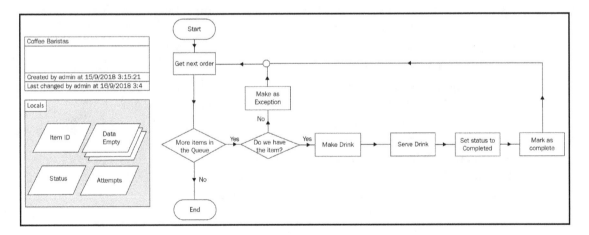

Re-run the **Coffee Cashiers** process to reload new orders into the queue. Finally, run the **Coffee Baristas** process again. Did all the orders complete successfully except for the ones that asked for tea? Look at the **Tags** column for that item; it should say **Exception: Item is out of stock**.

Tagging the item

Apart from recording down exception messages, the **Tags** column is also useful for labeling work queue items. Let's go back to our little example of the coffee shop. Suppose that you wanted to record special requests to perform an analysis of what people want to drink. To do so, you would need to label the orders as you take them. Let's observe the following steps to update the process to tag all special requests:

1. In the **Coffee Baristas** process, add a **Decision** stage in the **Yes** path of the **Do we have the item?** stage and configure it as follows:
   - **Name**: Is there a special request?
   - **Expression**: `[Data.Special Request]<>""`

   Here, we are checking the **Special Request** column to see whether it contains any information.

2. If there is a special request, we want to tag the work item. Drag an **Action** to the **Yes** path of the **Is there a special request?** stage and set its properties as follows:
   - **Name**: Record Special Requests
   - **Business Object**: Work Queues
   - **Action**: Tag Item

3. In the **Inputs** panel, fill in the following:
   - **Item ID**: Drag the Item ID data item from Data Explorer
   - **Tag**: `[Data.Special Request]`

   We just want to record whatever was specified in the special request column into the tag.

4. Link up the stages as shown in the following diagram:

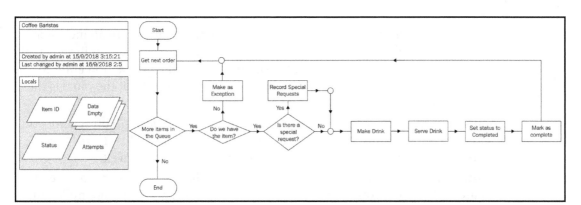

Finally, reload the order queue by running the **Coffee Cashiers** process. Then, run the **Coffee Baristas** process again. When it completes, look at the **Tags** column. The items with special requests now have that information recorded as Tags (see the following screenshot):

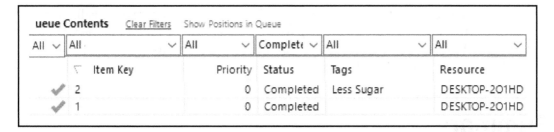

Filtering items

The idea behind tagging items is so that we can quickly query out the items that share the same tags. You can use the control room to filter the items by keying the keyword that you are looking for in the filter box. Let's try it out by observing the following steps:

1. Go back to the control room and click on **Queue Management | Coffee Shop**.
2. Click on the filter above the **Tags** column. Notice that you can enter any text you like in the box.
3. Go ahead and key in `Less Sugar`. The filter automatically shows only the work items tagged with `Less Sugar`.

The keywords could also be used for multiple conditions by specifying inclusion, exclusion, or multiple tags:

- **Inclusion tags**: Only finds items with the specific tag. You specify an inclusion tag by adding a plus sign in front of it. For example, +Less Sugar will return all items with less sugar as a special request. By default, all tags that you enter in the filter are inclusion tags. Therefore, entering **Less Sugar** (without the plus) is the same as entering +Less Sugar.
- **Exclusion tags**: Excludes any items that contain the specific tag. You specify an exclusion tag by adding a minus sign in front of it. For example, -Less Sugar will return all items that do not have less sugar as a special request.
- **Multiple tags**: Use a semi-colon to separate more than one tag. For example, if you are looking for work items that contain both less sugar and more milk, enter Less Sugar; More Milk as the filter criteria. Using multiple tags will always get work items that contain all the tags (also known as an AND condition). You can also mix in exclusion tags. +More Milk,-Less Sugar will return items that have special requests for *more milk* but not *less sugar*.

> You can use the filter expressions from within the process as well. Enter the tags that you are looking for in the **Tag Filter** property of the **Get Next Item** action. In this way, we can instruct the robot to only work on specific items within the queue.

Summary

In this chapter, we looked at the control room and saw how it can be used to run processes in unattended mode. We scheduled a robot to run at a specific date and time without the need for a human to trigger it. We also studied work queues by creating our own coffee shop process to add orders to a queue, mark each order as completed/exception, and to update the status as the drink progresses through the order system.

In the final chapter of this book, we will round up by looking at how we can handle exceptions.

11
Exception Handling

In a perfect world, robots would run perfectly every day. Unfortunately, this is the real world, and there will be times when robots encounter situations that they are not familiar with. When that happens, a robot will terminate the process with an error message. That is called an exception. What should we do when an exception happens?

In this chapter, we will cover the basics of exception handling. We will do the following:

- Catch exceptions gracefully
- Handle errors with exception routines
- Take a look at the logs to figure out exactly which stage terminated

Expected and unexpected exceptions

So far, we have tried to program the process with the happy path in mind. For example, in the **Weekly purchase of groceries** process, we got the robot to read the shopping list, look for the item on the Amazon site, and added it to the shopping cart. As you ran the Weekly purchasing of groceries process (as above), did you encounter any exceptions?

Exceptions may be expected or unexpected. Sometimes, we are able to predict the kind of errors that the robot may encounter. Some examples of expected exceptions are as follows:

- The **Add to Cart** button is disabled. Amazon may not ship the product to the country in which you reside, or the product is out of stock, or perhaps the robot just does not understand the purchasing scheme of the product (for instance, you have to buy two items instead of one).
- The search was not able to locate the product.
- The Excel shopping list could not be located.

Before building a process, it's a good idea to look through each step and see whether you are able to think ahead and prepare the robot for more exceptions. The more you are able to anticipate the problems that the robot may face, the more stable your process is going to be when its deployed to production.

Inevitably, no matter how much effort has been put into the thought process, there may be exceptions that are not anticipated. These usually fall into the *we don't know what we don't know* bucket. Some of these include the following:

- We allocated five seconds for the Amazon site to load. Network conditions may deteriorate, causing the site to take more than the usual time to load completely.
- Amazon decides to perform an overhaul of its user interface. The **Search** and **Add to Cart** buttons may change property values and the robot is not able to identify them.

You may be thinking that since we are able to articulate what these *unexpected* exceptions are, they are really *expected*. The truth is, there is very little that we can do when such a situation happens. For example, if we increase the expected load time of the Amazon site, how much do we want to increase it by—to 10 seconds? What if that is still not enough? Therefore, the robot is usually not able to handle these errors.

Raising exceptions

We use the **Exception** stage (⬜) whenever we want to alert the robot when a process is not going the right way. For example, earlier, when we built the **Amazon - Search** business object, we added a few wait stages to watch for certain elements on the page before we interacted with them. If there were problems, such as should the product page not load, we raised an exception, as shown in the following diagram:

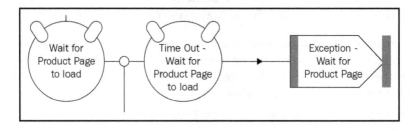

When raising an exception, we may add details about the error, as shown here:

- **Exception type** helps to categorize the exception. You can select from a predefined drop-down list or enter a type of your own. If you choose to add a new type, it will be subsequently added to the drop-down list.
- **Exception detail** provides the space to enter the full descriptive text of the error. In our example, we used it to say that the product page could not be loaded within the specified time.
- **Preserve the type and detail of the current exception** Check this box if you want to preserve the internal error message type and detail.
- **Save screen capture** will take a screen shot of the screen at the time the error occurred and store it in the logs. This is very useful for troubleshooting later, especially when the robot is running in unattended mode.

Handling exceptions

Raising exceptions is great for alerting the robot when things are not going well. How then should the robot respond? When we ran the process from Studio, and if an exception was encountered, the process terminated with a pop-up dialog. The dialog contains the error type and detail, shown as follows:

To dismiss, the dialog, we simply clicked the **OK** button. However, the process has terminated. And in order to get it working again, we have to re-run the process.

A better way would be to see whether the robot is able to handle the error and continue running the rest of the process. Say, if the product page did not load, perhaps it could do the following:

- Wait a few seconds before retrying
- Retry for a fixed number of times before giving up
- Record the error message somewhere, like in an error log, and email a human that something has gone wrong

The recover stage

The recover stage is represented by a pentagon ⬠. When an exception is raised, the process will first attempt to jump to the first recover stage within the same block. Should it not find any, then it will look for a recover block on the same subpage. If it can't find any, then it will look for a recover stage on the **Main** page. If no recover stages are found, the process will simply terminate. This process of looking for recover stages from the subpage to the **Main** page is called bubbling.

Once in the recover stage, the process is in *exception mode*. At this point, you will execute steps to attempt to handle the error.

The resume stage

As soon as the error has been gracefully handled, you may want to continue with the rest of the main process. In order to do so, you will have to add in the resume stage (⬠). This will negate the error, and the process will move back to being in the *non-exception mode*.

Using the recover and resume stages to gracefully handle exceptions

Let's program the robot to record the error message by use of the recover and resume stages:

- From Blue Prism Studio, open the **Amazon - Search** business object for editing. Open the **Add to Cart** action.
- Drag a **Recover** stage and drop it somewhere near the **End** stage. Rename it from `Recover1` to `Recover`.
- Drag a **Calculation** stage and drop it beneath the **Recover** stage. Configure it as follows:
  - **Name**: `Set Success to False`
  - **Expression**: `False`
  - **Store Result in**: `Success`
  - Drag a **Resume** stage and drop it beneath the **Set Success to False** stage
  - Rename it from `Resume1` to `Resume`
- Finally, link up all the stages, as shown in the following diagram:

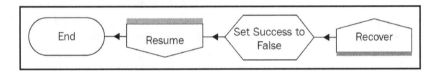

Now run the process again. This time, if there is an exception raised in the **Add to Cart** action, notice that the process jumps to the **Recover** stage. It will set the **Success** flag to False before resuming to process the remaining items in the list.

Using blocks to group stages that share a common error handling routine

In the preceding example, we demonstrated a simple use case of how to use the recover and resume stages. Take a look at the other parts of the **Weekly purchase of groceries** process. Which are the parts that tend to break and cause the process to terminate unexpectedly?

Perhaps you may have noticed that most of the exceptions happen in the **Search** and **Add Item to Cart** actions, especially within the loop that processes the items, for example, if the Amazon site failed to load, or if the search yielded zero results? The process still throws up the error message and terminates. It becomes especially frustrating, for example if you have 10 items to purchase and an error occurs while trying to purchase the fourth item, the process terminates and leaves the fifth to tenth items out of the cart. What would be ideal is for the process to continue with the fifth item. To do so, we need to handle the error gracefully. We will record the error details and move on to the next item.

To do so, we will use blocks. Earlier, we used blocks to organize our data items. We used them to draw a box around data items that share the same scope. We did that purely for organizational purposes to make it easier to look for data items and to improve the diagram's readability. Blocks have another important use. They are also used to group stages that share a common error handling routine.

Let's see how we can use blocks to handle the errors that occur within the loop that processes the items:

- From Blue Prism Studio, open the **Weekly purchase of groceries** process. Open the **Search and Add Item to Cart** page for editing.
- Add a new text data item to the page. Give it the name `ErrorMessage`. We will use it to store the details of any error that occurs when adding an item to the cart.
- Draw a block that envelopes the **Launch Amazon**, **Search**, **Add to Cart** and **Close Amazon** stages, as shown in the following diagram. Name the block **Processing Items**. The block is used to indicate that we will only be handling errors that happen within these stages:

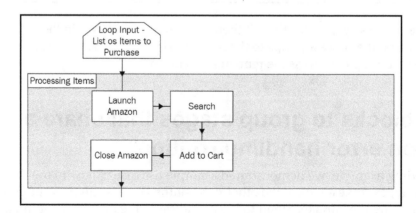

- Drag and drop a **Recover** stage onto the diagram. Rename the stage from **Recover1** to **Recover**.

- Add a **Calculation** stage beneath the **Recover** stage. Name the stage **Set Success=False**. Here, we will set the **Success** flag to `false`. Configure it as follows:
    - **Name**: Set `Success = False`
    - **Expression**: `False`
    - **Store Result In**: `Success`

- Next, add another **Calculation** stage and configure it as follows. In this stage, we will record the error details in the `ErrorMessage` data item:
    - **Name**: `Record Error Details`
    - **Expression**: `ExceptionDetail()`
    - **Store Result In**: `ErrorMessage`

- Whenever we are not able to add the item to the basket, we will add the full error message to the status. Double-click on the `Status=Failed` calculation stage and change the expression to the following: `"Failed to add item to cart. Details:" & [ErrorMessage]`

- Drag a **Resume** stage and drop it beneath the **Record Error Details** stage.

- Finally, link up all the stages, as shown in the following screenshot. Notice that we have linked the **Resume** stage to the point before we record the item's status. This means that should there be any errors while processing the item, we are able to record the error message before moving on to the next item:

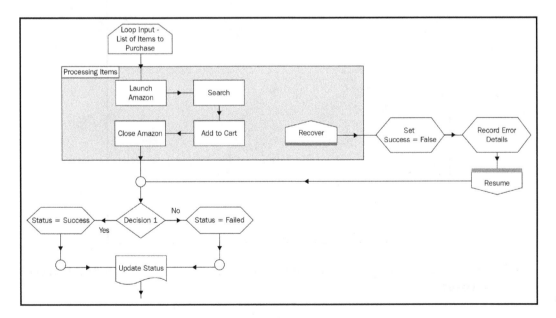

Handling unexpected errors

Despite our best efforts to anticipate, catch, and handle all the errors that we can think of, there will always be a chance that the process will encounter an error that we have not foreseen and will terminate unexpectedly. When an unexpected error occurs, the usual protocol is for the robot to inform the human in charge of the process that it is not able to continue, the exact point where it stopped, and when it terminated.

The best place to catch all unexpected errors is the **Main** page. Remember that exception handling bubbles up from business objects to subpages and finally to the **Main** page. It does not matter where in the process the exception occurs; an error handling routine on the Main page will catch it.

Let's add stages to the **Main** page of the **Weekly purchase of groceries** process to handle any error that has not been specifically dealt with in the subpages. When an exception occurs, we will send an email to the administrator informing them of the error details:

1. In the **Weekly purchase of groceries** process, open the **Main** page for editing.
2. Draw a block around the stages between the **Start** and **End** stages, as shown in the following diagram. For clarity, give the block the label **Main**:

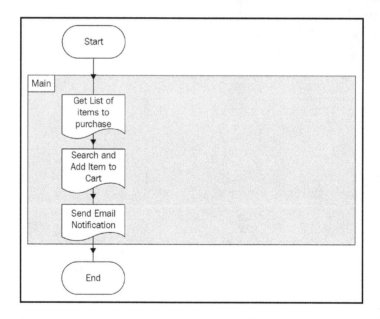

3. Drag a **Recover** stage and place it within the **Block**. Rename it from **Recover1** to **Recover**.

4. Drag an **Action** stage and drop it beneath the **Recover** stage. Make sure that it is outside the **Block**. We will use the **MS Outlook Email VBO** object to send an email to the administrator. Configure the action as follows:
   - **Name**: Email Alert
   - **Business object**: MS Outlook Email VBO
   - **Action**: Send Email

In the **Inputs** panel, set the following property values:

- **To**: admin@somewhere.com (you might want to replace this with your own email address)
- **Subject**: "[Error] Weekly purchase of groceries"
- **Message**: ExceptionStage() & ":" & ExceptionDetail()

5. Drag a **Resume** stage and drop it beneath the **Email Alert** stage. Rename it from Resume1 to Resume.
6. Link up all the stages as shown here:

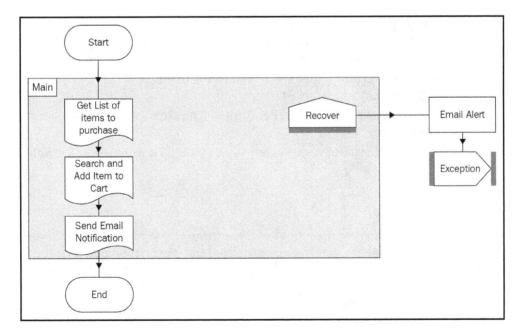

So now we have completed adding exception handling routines to the process. Save the process and close it.

Debugging and troubleshooting from the control room

So far, we have been running the process by clicking on the **Play** button. We get to see exactly what the robot is doing on the screen and Studio highlights the stage it is at. If there are any issues, we simply pause the process and investigate the stages where the error occurs. However, when the process has been deployed to a production robot, it is likely that all you will get is a message from the control room that the process has either completed or terminated. How then can we troubleshoot to figure out exactly what happened and where the problem occurred?

Recap – running the process from the control room

Let's try running our completed process from the room and see whether we can make sense of the messages that are recorded there when the process completes its run:

1. From Blue Prism Studio, click **Control**.
2. From the **Available Processes** panel, drag **Weekly purchase of groceries** and drop it into the **Resource** that represents your computer in the right-hand panel.
3. An orange-colored entry appears in the **Environment** panel at the bottom. Right-click on the session and select **Start**.
4. The process status changes from **Pending** to **Running**. Wait for the process to complete its run.
5. When its done, the status should show up as either **Terminated** or **Completed**.

Log viewer

How can we see a record of what the robot has done through the control room? Thankfully, Blue Prism records all the stages that have been carried out by the robot, all the inputs as well as the outputs. By looking at the record, we are able to piece together the full process, without watching the robot at work. This is extremely important for troubleshooting. In the real world, we can't afford to sit in front of the robot and watch it 24/7. Should the process terminate, we need be able to look at the logs to see what happened.

The logs are available in **Log Viewer**. To access it from the control room, simply right-click on the session that you want to investigate and select **View Log** from the context menu. Let's take a look at the logs from the session that we have just triggered:

1. From **Control Room**, observe the **Environment** panel at the bottom. The session that we have just triggered is listed with a status of either **Completed** or **Terminated**.

2. Right-click anywhere on the session's row and choose **View Log** from the context menu.

3. The **Session Log Viewer** appears in a new window.

4. To get the most information out of the **Session Log Viewer**, right-click anywhere and choose **Show All Columns** from the context menu. All available columns are now displayed. Here's what we see on our screen:

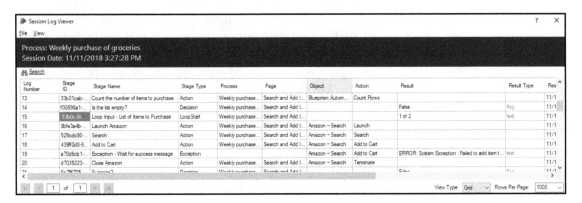

> There's quite a bit of information on display in the Log Viewer. To make the screen bigger, drag the corners of the window to expand it. Once you have increased the window's size, press *F5* to refresh its contents, and the table will automatically expand to fill up the larger space.

5. The information displayed is a text-based version of exactly what happened when the robot ran the process. Here's a brief description of each column:

   - **Log Number**: A running number that shows the sequence of events.
   - **Stage ID**: A unique identifier for each stage. Useful for distinguishing stages that share the same name.
   - **Stage Name**: The name that was given to the stage when we built the process. This is why it is important to give stages meaningful and unique names. It makes reading the logs a lot easier when we need to troubleshoot.

- **Stage Type**: The stage's type (for example, **Action**, **Decision**, and **Choice**).
- **Process**: The name of the process that is running.
- **Page**: The name of the page that is running.
- **Object**: The name of the object that is executing. Applies only to parts of the process where an object is called.
- **Action**: The name of the action that is executing. Applies only to parts of the process where an object is called.
- **Result**: The output of the action.
  - For decisions, it records whether the result is True or False
  - For calculations, it records the result of the expression.
  - For loop start and ends, it records the item that it is working on. For example, 1 of 2 means that it is working on the first item out of a collection that contains two items.
  - If an error occurs, the error details are also recorded in the **Result** column.
- **Result Type**: Indicates whether the value stored in the **Result** column is a **Text**, **Flag**, or **Number**.
- **Resource Start**: The date and time when the stage started execution.
- **Resource End**: The date and time when the stage ended execution.
- **Parameters**: The values contained in all input and output parameters of the stage.

As you can see, the logs contains a stage-by-stage account of the entire run. Without watching the robot opening screens and clicking buttons, we are able to piece together the exact steps it took when running the process.

Controlling what gets logged

All the information is logged into the Blue Prism database. As time goes by, the database may get choked with too much information, resulting in lags and performance issues. It is important to control what information gets logged and what does not. Ideally, we keep minimal information required for troubleshooting. It is always a question of striking a balance between what is needed and what it is good to have.

By default, logging is enabled for all stages when we drag them onto the canvas. You can turn logging on or off in the following ways:

1. From Process (or Object) Studio, select **Edit | All Stages**. A context menu appears with the following options:
    - **Enable logging**: Turns on logging for all stages in the process/object.
    - **Disable logging**: Turns off logging for all stages in the process/object.
    - **Log errors only**: Only logs when an error has occurred.
2. Alternatively, edit the properties of individual stages. There is a **Stage logging** drop-down list at the bottom of each stage that controls the logging (refer to the following screenshot). You can also toggle the logging of the input and output parameters by checking the **Don't log parameters on this stage** box:

Deciding what gets logged is often an afterthought. However, with careful planning, this exercise can be brought to the front of the design phase. In this way, we can plan upfront what data is captured in the logs and what is not. We are then able to design exception messages and types that will make sense to the people reading the logs.

Another important consideration is to not log data in production. You may have security requirements in your organization, whereby the people who have access to the logs are not supposed to access production data. In such cases, we have to control what gets logged with more care. If someone unwittingly logs sensitive data, you can be sure that the company auditors will be on the robot's case soon.

Searching for errors

For processes with many stages, there is an easier way to scan through the list for the line that you may be looking for. A common scenario is when the process terminates and you want to find out exactly where in the process it stopped.

To do so, use the search function. The **Search** button is located at the top right-hand corner of the **Session Log Viewer** (see the following screenshot). Click on the **Search** button to reveal the **Search panel**:

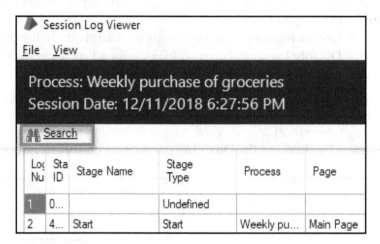

There are two ways to get the search results, and these are explained here:

- **Using the Find Next button**: To look for errors one by one, enter the error keyword into the **Find** box. Click **Find Next**. The next cell that contains the word error gets highlighted in red. Continue to use the **Find Next** button to look for more cells that contain the error text.
- **Using the Find All button**: Another useful way to search through the logs is to use the **Find All** button. With the error keyword in the search box, try clicking on the **Find All** button. All the cells that contain the word error are highlighted in red. If the log is split into multiple pages, you can scroll through the pages to look at all the cells that have been highlighted.

Exporting to Excel

There are times where you may want to export the entire log to Excel for further analysis. To do so, observe the following steps:

1. From the top menu in **Session Log Viewer**, select **File | Export Entire Log**.
2. You will be prompted to save the log file in either a CSV, text, or HTML file. If you wish to open the file in Excel, choose **CSV** and click **Next**.

3. Click **Browse** to choose the location on the computer to save the file to. Notice that the file name automatically suggested by Blue Prism is simply `BPA Complete Session Log.csv`. You can choose to rename the file to a name of your choice. When you are done, click **Next**.

The file gets exported. When completed, you can navigate to the file and open it up in Excel. From there, you have the full suite of Excel productivity tools to extract the data that you need (for example, using *Ctrl +F* to look for the word *error*). You can also file the document for archival purposes.

Summary

In this chapter, we completed the process by adding exception handling routines to take care of the errors that we anticipate, as well as the errors that we don't expect. If the process should terminate for whatever reason, the robot will send an email to a human to notify them that there is an issue. It will also provide information about where it stopped and why.

We also covered the log viewer, which keeps a record of all the stages that the robot has executed. This is often used in troubleshooting the process when it runs in unattended mode. We looked at how we can turn logging on or off, search for keywords in the log, and even export it to Excel for further analysis.

Other Books You May Enjoy

If you enjoyed this book, you may be interested in these other books by Packt:

Learning Robotic Process Automation

Alok Mani Tripathi

ISBN: 978-1-78847-094-0

- Understand Robotic Process Automation technology
- Learn UiPath programming techniques to deploy robot configurations
- Explore various data extraction techniques
- Learn about integrations with various popular applications such as SAP and MS Office
- Debug a programmed robot including logging and exception handling
- Maintain code version and source control
- Deploy and control Bots with UiPath Orchestrator

Leave a review - let other readers know what you think

Please share your thoughts on this book with others by leaving a review on the site that you bought it from. If you purchased the book from Amazon, please leave us an honest review on this book's Amazon page. This is vital so that other potential readers can see and use your unbiased opinion to make purchasing decisions, we can understand what our customers think about our products, and our authors can see your feedback on the title that they have worked with Packt to create. It will only take a few minutes of your time, but is valuable to other potential customers, our authors, and Packt. Thank you!

Index